Spiders
and
Snakes
and
Rats—
Oh My!

A Humorous Account of Over Forty Years of Nature Education

Scott Lee

Fulton Books, Inc.
Meadville, PA

Published by Fulton Books 2021

ISBN 978-1-64952-599-4 (paperback)
ISBN 978-1-64952-600-7 (digital)

Printed in the United States of America

Contents

Part One

• •

A Little History

Before we get started, I thought it might be
helpful to see where I got started.

Chapter 1
Family History

I was born and raised in a small town near the western coastline (Mississippi River) of Wisconsin. Holmen only had 634 people when I graduated in a class of seventy-six students. We had a small cottage that sat up on brick stilts right on the Mississippi in Trempealeau, about eleven miles from Holmen, and we spent our summers there. I had an incredibly happy childhood, blessed with the best parents one could ever ask for and four terrific sisters (I was the only boy) that were five, six, and seven years older and two years younger. My mom was an elementary teacher and my dad, the manager of a small creamery in Holmen, was an avid outdoorsman who loved to hunt, fish, and hike; so I guess from the very beginning, I was destined to go in the direction I did. I hope my parents realized just how grateful I am to them for raising me the way they did and being such positive influences in my life.

I learned many valuable, lifelong lessons from both Mom and Dad. I hunted, fished, and hiked with Dad often. The first time I was old enough to carry a gun, he took me deer hunting. We had a doe permit so I would have a choice of shooting either a doe or buck (most places were "buck only" back then unless you were lucky enough to get a doe permit). Anyway, not too long into the hunt, three deer approached us. A nice big doe stopped close enough to us that even my twelve-year-old shooting skills wouldn't have been an issue in hitting my target. I patiently awaited the "okay" from Dad to shoot, but it never came. I watched disappointedly as the three deer wandered off, wondering why Dad never had me shoot what would have been my very first deer. He very gently told me that the other two deer were undoubtedly the fawns of the big doe so it would have been cruel to kill their mother—certainly a lesson on compassion I carried with me my entire life.

One of the first time I was old enough to hunt on my own, I had hiked up into the woods only a few blocks from our house to hunt deer. After a few hours of seeing nothing, I headed home. Before leaving the woods, I came across a blue jay sitting on a branch above me. I decided to test my skills on him and successfully "blew him away." Dad later asked how the hunt had gone, so I relayed to him my lack of success but that I'd taken out my frustrations on the blue jay. My dad really never got angry with me, but there was no doubt about his disappointment in me for shooting the blue jay. He told me there is no reason to shoot any creature just for the sake of killing it and that I had no reason to kill the bird. Again, the lesson on compassion, but also learning to value all wildlife was passed on to me that day. An even greater lesson I learned that day is that anger is not the most effective way to handle situations. I knew that I never ever wanted to disappoint my dad again—and, although not perfect, I think I did a pretty good job of that through my life. (I did go through the teenage years, however, so know I failed a number of times during those days.)

I'd often complain about having only sisters, but deep down I've always known how lucky I was. I guess I was kind of spoiled, but I sure hope that never showed—at least in a negative way. I know all four of them loved me as much as I loved them, although when the three older ones were dressing me up or making me polka, waltz, and schottische with them or treating me like "one of the girls," I wasn't all that crazy about them. My younger sister and I, despite having plenty of arguments and spats, always had a special bond (and being so close in age, I always enjoyed her pretty friends coming around, and she seemed to enjoy my good-looking friends when they were around—a win-win for us, I guess, especially in our teenage years).

I developed a theory as I aged that "I was the only sibling that Mom and Dad really planned." I had it all figured out! Sally was born only a year after they were married, so she was obviously an accident. Dad was drafted and went into the army and World War II shortly after, and I often heard stories about the neighbors feeling sorry for Mom as she got pregnant whenever Dad came home on leave. Obviously, then, both Susan and Mary were also accidents.

With Dad being who he is, I know he was aching to have a son to share all his sporting and outdoor activities (wasn't so common back then for the girls to get as involved in those things). After the war and getting settled into his career, therefore, he/they decided it was time to try once more and get that son that Dad so craved and—presto—along came me! I was definitely planned! Two years later, Janie showed up—another girl—so there's no doubt that she was yet another accident. Why would they want more kids? Anyway, well into my adulthood, I presented this theory to Mom, saying, "I was the only child you planned, wasn't I?" She simply smiled (she did *lots* of that!) and said, "No, there was no such thing as planning back in those days. You were *all* accidents!" ☹ I could never get her to admit it, but I still think that I was the only planned one!

The Lee Family (1959)

Chapter 2
Career History

After a pretty successful high school career, barely sliding through four years of college with a double major in sociology and psychology at Luther College in Decorah, Iowa, reconnecting with Judy (my "first love" and high school sweetheart), getting married a month after college graduation, and putting in four-plus months on active duty with the US Army Reserve (starting only a month after our wedding), my career finally got started. I worked as a childcare worker in a home for kids that had been through a lot of tough times where many of them were having lots of troubles getting through life. I loved my work there, but after a couple of years, I realized that some burnout was setting in. I always knew that I wanted to work with kids, but knew I needed to change my career path if that was going to continue to be rewarding to me. I, therefore, went back to school to get my Elementary Education certificate. I knew my double major in sociology and psychology wasn't going to get me where I wanted to go. After two years of going to school full-time, as well as continuing to work at the children's home full-time, I got my Bachelor of Science degree in Elementary Education (certified in grades one through six) at Winona State University in Winona, Minnesota, and landed the best teaching position I could ever have imagined.

I started teaching fifth grade at Trempealeau Elementary School in the town where I had spent every summer of my life—a community I loved more than anyplace in the world, and that love has continued to grow to this day. My career got off to a rather auspicious start as the chain came off my motorcycle on my way to my very first day—a teacher in-service—and I was going to be late. I basically threw my cycle into the ditch and flagged down the first car to come along—not thumb-out hitchhiking, but rather an all-out waving of the arms. Luckily, it was a high school teacher in the district, and he saved my career by getting me there on time. Whew! I taught there for thirty-three years, always with a fifth-grade homeroom. I've thanked my mom often for showing me what a rewarding profession this is.

Along the way, my dad's influence made its way into my teaching, and I started attending workshops and conferences related to our natural world. I became a life member of Wisconsin Association for Environmental Education (WAEE) and went to several of their offerings every year. Dad had taught me the love of our environment and natural world, and WAEE showed me how to take that love and help my students learn to love and appreciate it. Although teaching elementary school involves teaching everything, I found a way to integrate environmental education and learning about our natural world into every subject. I also eventually picked up my master's degree (ME-PD) at University of Wisconsin-La Crosse in La Crosse, Wisconsin, focusing on Environmental Education and Natural Science, which was also a great help. I incorporated field trips in as often as I was allowed (I sure loved being outside a lot more than being restricted to the classroom). Being in Trempealeau, I had access to the Mississippi River only a few blocks from school, the river bluffs and Perrot State Park just a short distance away, and also Trempealeau National Wildlife Refuge just a ways beyond that. I couldn't have asked for a more ideal place to teach the way I wanted to teach with all those resources so close at hand.

View of Trempealeau and Lock & Dam Six
Trempealeau Elementary School at left center
(Photo taken from first / Liberty Peak above Trempealeau)

Most of the stories that follow are related to actual experiences I had in my thirty-three years of teaching fifth graders about our natural world. I did go on, after retiring from Trempealeau Elementary, to teach two sections of the Introduction to Environmental Studies for eight years at the University of Wisconsin-La Crosse. This was another wonderful experience and a great way to more slowly wind down my career. Some of these stories may also apply to my college teaching experience. I'd generally start out my first day of each semester by telling my students, "I had thirty-three years of experience with fifth graders but am much less experienced with college age, so you should expect to be treated more like fifth graders," and I did just that! I think the great majority of them liked it that way, and we had a lot of fun—and I think they may have even learned a few things. They likely ended up "smarter than a fifth grader," although I had some pretty smart fifth graders through the years in Trempealeau, especially in the nature/environment areas.

Part Two

• •

Stories and Experiences

Now on to the fun stuff!

Chapter 3
Eat S--t?

One of my favorite activities to do while hiking with groups is what I call a "nonnature hike" (*see* sheet of possible items on following pages). If possible, I will go out ahead and place certain objects that don't apparently relate to nature in strategic locations and have the groups try to explain what that object has to do with where they find it. For example, I might place a fork next to a dandelion plant. They hopefully will reason it out that we can eat dandelion, which is true—leaves, buds, and flower as a salad, roots can be ground up to make a coffee-like beverage (I didn't go into the potential for dandelion wine with kids' groups, but those college kids' ears seemed to perk up when I mentioned it!). A glass jar can be placed in the sand as glass is made from sand, a syrup container by a maple tree, a phone by a dead tree (woodpeckers not only beat on the trees to get food but also to communicate their territory to other woodpeckers), etc.

One common plant I usually find along the way is called mullein. It has rather large leaves that are very velvety in texture. They tend to have trouble remembering the name mullein, but when I tell them that its nickname is "nature's or hunter's toilet paper," they remember! It really is as "soft as Charmin," very common, and stays soft like that well into the winter. After finding the mullein, I try to find a deer trail or some other deer sign (buck rub, scrap, tracks, or signs of browsing). Then comes my favorite "prop" where I'll put a roll of toilet paper beside some "deer droppings." I then talk about the scat decaying, bringing nutrients back into the soil, etc. I also go into this big speech on the digestive system of the deer—the "fact" that the food goes through the deer so quickly (they actually do "go" an average of thirteen times a day) that when the solid waste comes out, it still has many vitamins and nutrients still present in it. It is therefore edible as a survival food. This, obviously, grosses them out, but when I actually pick some up, they are really disgusted! That's nothing, however, compared to the reaction when I plop one into my mouth and start chewing! The variety of reactions is priceless. Needless to say, I make it very clear eventually that deer droppings are *not* edible, so "don't try this at home"—at least not with real droppings! I have planted chocolate covered raisins, which are pretty much a dead ringer for real deer droppings and would undoubtedly taste a whole lot better!

I wish I could remember them all, but I've had many wonderful quotes through my years of doing this activity:

My nephew's comment after his mother, who was "in" on it, ate one, "Yuch! I will never kiss you again. I won't kiss anyone with poop breath!"

A teacher at a workshop I was leading, "Do you realize what kind of parasites might be in them?"

To which I responded, "Well, I suppose, but I never eat very many so I should be okay."

When hiking with another sister, my two young children, knowing all about the ruse, asked, "Are these the good kind to eat, Dad?" I told them they were, so they each ate one. When my sister actually started eating them while still thinking they were droppings, I gave her "crap" about it.

She commented, "Well, I knew you wouldn't let your kids eat them if they weren't good for you."

And after trying one, and still believing they actually are deer droppings, I invariably get a comment such as, "Wow, they really are good. They even taste kind of like chocolate!"

The common response, however, is generally one of disgust, revulsion, covering up their eyes, and turning their backs.

I'd also find and taste deer droppings with my college students. Wow, do they ever get grossed out! It was especially effective with my fall classes, as we'd hike and find them within the first couple of weeks so they didn't know me very well yet. I'm sure many couldn't wait to get to the registrar's office to transfer out of my class. We'd do it toward the end of the spring class so they had gotten to know me by then and likely found it hard to believe much of anything I'd tell them. When I'd first find the scat, I'd give them a little poetry lesson:

It begins with "S" and it ends with "T."
It comes out of you, and it comes out of me.
I know what you're thinking...and it might be called that...
But be scientific and call it SCAT.

Back in the classroom the next time, I'd bring lots of edible scat samples for them, all packaged up in ziplock bags, and pass them around to sample. Among the special treats would be bunny bowel movement (cocoa puffs), mouse manure (chocolate sprinkles), Girl Scout scat (thin mints), deer droppings (chocolate-covered raisins), fawn feces (the smaller chocolate-covered raisins), worm waste (gummy worms), fish fecal matter (goldfish crackers), teacher turds (alphabets cereal), goat grunt (caramels), snowman shit (marshmallows), cupid's calling card (small candy hearts), Santa's sittings (chocolate-covered marshmallow Santas), great pumpkin's poo poo (orange pumpkin candy), leprechaun crap (small hard green candy), coyote crap (doggy bone biscuits)—stroll through the candy section and let your imagination be your guide. I've also given assortments of these "treats" to friends and family—makes great Christmas presents for those hard to buy for. ☺

Coyote Crap
(Photo taken in Yellowstone's Lamar Valley)

Nonnature Hike

The following items can be preplaced or carried along and placed by the appropriate natural objects that you are able to identify to later be "found" on your hike.

Have hikers explain what each object might have to do with the natural object it is by.

Tea Bag/Box
  - wild mint (Tea can be made from mint. Rub the leaves or flower between your fingers to bring out the minty smell. Notice that mint always will have a square stem. Goldenrod or yarrow can also be used to make a tea but neither are as tasty.)

Band-Aid
  - next to plantain (This is a common backyard "weed" that was used by the Native Americans and early pioneers as a cure for minor cuts and rashes, such as poison ivy or stinging nettle. The juice from scrunching up the leaf can be rubbed on the irritation, or it can be used as a poultice.)

Fork or Spoon
  - by dandelion, nuts, berries, plantain, nettle, mushrooms, etc. Dandelion (leaves and flower are edible, and the roots can be ground up to make "coffee." The name comes from a French word pronounced "dent day lay own," meaning tooth of the lion—look at the edge of the leaf). Nuts (acorns, hickory, walnut). Berries, plantain (can be eaten as a salad as well as used as medicine). Stinging nettle (leaves are edible—little hairs on the stem is what causes the skin irritation). Mushrooms (such as puffball, morel, sulfur shelf, or shaggy mane and numerous others).

Toilet Paper
- by mullein (Mullein has large, very soft leaves—like Charmin. The first year of growth for the plant is low to the ground, but the second year, a long stalk grows up the middle to a height of four to five feet, and the top is covered with little yellow flowers mid- to late summer. Its nickname is "nature's toilet paper" for obvious reasons. The leaves can often be found still green throughout the fall and even through much of the winter; therefore, "hunter's toilet paper" is also an appropriate nickname.)

Wood Spoons (Made of Bamboo in China)
- hang from or lean against a tree (Trees are used to make it. As the spoons are made from a rain forest tree, it can lead to a discussion on how buying these can encourage destruction of rain forests.)

Allergy Meds
- hang from goldenrod (Goldenrod is often blamed for allergy problems, but it is actually given a "bad rap," as it is the ragweed that often grows in the same areas that cause the problems. Because goldenrod is blooming in bright yellow/gold colors at the time ragweed is causing the allergy problems, people often falsely attribute the allergies to goldenrod.)

Fishing Bobber
- also on goldenrod (Watch for "galls"—a wide, cancer-like growth on the stem, growing on the stems of goldenrod. There's an insect that lays its egg on the stem, and the plant grows out around it, leaving what looks like a ball on the stem. The egg will hatch into the larva stage, and it eats itself out of the gall. If there's no hole in the side, the larva is likely inside, so cut it open to reveal the white larva. If there is a small hole, it has already eaten its way out. If there is a large hole, a bird such as the chickadee, has pecked its way in for an easy meal.)

Telephone
- on or next to a dead tree (Woodpeckers will not only peck on the tree looking for an insect meal burrowed inside but also pound on them to "communicate" to others where their individual territories are.)

Toilet Paper
- on deer trail by deer droppings (You can discuss the digestive systems of animals. Deer "go" about thirteen times a day, so this can be used to determine deer populations. Also, the value of this as a "fertilizer" for the soil can be talked about. As mentioned earlier, you can also have some fun with it by "eating" it.)

Horseshoe
- by clover (Talk about superstitions—horseshoes and four-leaf clovers as good luck; black cats, broken mirrors, walking under a ladder as bad luck, etc.)

Strawberry Jam Container
- by wild strawberry plant (Wild strawberries are much smaller than store-bought but taste just as sweet and are found in early summer.)

Sunglasses
- by a white birch tree (You can make sunglasses from the white bark by slitting holes and tying them on with string. White will reflect much of the glare away from the eyes. This can be an important "survival" tool in winter to prevent snow blindness.)

Grape Jam Container
- by wild grape vines (Wild grapes are much smaller than store-bought, taste much more sour, and are *not* seedless. The berries are green at first but turn dark purple when

ripe in late summer. Despite the tartness, they make a very good grape jam with the help of sugar, of course.)

Glass Jar
- in the sand (Glass is made of sand, which makes it a good container to use as we have an unlimited supply of sand. Encourage recycling, however, as glass does not decompose. Talk about paper also being a good container as trees are a renewable resource, but plastic and Styrofoam are bad as they are oil-based—a nonrenewable.)

Crown
- hang on Queen Ann's lace (This is a very common white flowering plant that will grow in disturbed areas—areas that have been mowed or farmed such as along roadsides or under highline wires.)

Maple Syrup Container
- by a maple tree (Syrup is made from the sap of maple trees—especially sugar maples.)

Ginger Container
- next to wild ginger plant (The roots are ground up to make the spice. It has the heart-shaped leaf and grows close to the ground in wooded areas.)

Paper
- by a tree (Paper is made from trees—good one to start with as it is easy. If placed by a birch tree, you can talk about birch bark being used by early people as paper, therefore, the name paper birch.)

Skull and Crossbones
- poison ivy (The oil on the leaves and stems of poison ivy is what causes the irritation if you have an allergy to it. Usually, it can be prevented if you wash with soap and

water within an hour or two as it does not immediately cause problems.
- stinging nettle (The hairy particles on the stem of stinging nettle is what causes skin irritation. It will generally go away within about seven minutes if you don't scratch it. The leaves are okay to touch and can actually be eaten as a salad.)

Rope
- also on stinging nettle (You can boil the stems to get rid of the little hairlike particles that cause the skin irritation. Its fiber is very strong so it can then be used as a rope or to make bracelets or necklaces.)

Brush
- in a pine tree (Native Americans and early pioneers used pine needles to brush their hair.)

Litter
- anywhere (This can be used to talk about the negative effects people can have on our environment. It may only be one small piece of paper but multiply that times the billions of people on this earth and it becomes a very large problem.)

Scouring Pad
- next to scouring rush plant (This is a prehistoric plant and would likely be the oldest living thing you'd find. It was used by early pioneers to scrub and clean dishes, etc. as it has a rough texture.)

This is about a one-hour hike if you discuss approximately twelve to fourteen of the above items. Let your imagination be your guide to substitute other items.

Chapter 4
Worm Cookies

Some years I did a fairly extensive wild foods unit with my kids, but would always point out various wild, edible foods while hiking. The "nonnature hike" previously mentioned always included several. One of those wild foods we'd talk about was worms. I'd also read the book *How to Eat Fried Worms* to them, a cute and funny book that involves losing a bet between a couple of boys, forcing one to have to eat a number of worms over a period of time. I talk about the fact that you can actually eat worms, emphasizing the fact that the word "edible" isn't necessarily a synonym of "yummy." Worms are like 99 percent protein (and 1 percent dirt?), so won't likely hurt you—but might make you gag or throw up!

One year, I decided to make chocolate chip earthworm cookies. I actually boiled some worms, fried them in butter, and then cut them into small pieces. My mom had the absolute best oatmeal chocolate chip cookie recipe, so I mixed them up and stirred in the worm pieces. I then baked them, brought them to school, and put them in the staff lounge. I put a note on them saying, "These cookies do have an ingredient in them that isn't normally in cookies, but it won't hurt you. Try them if you want." They all disappeared like any treat does in the lounge. Everyone said they were really good, and many asked what the secret ingredient was. I was tempted to tell, but then an elderly teacher, who wasn't necessarily known for her sense of humor, ate two of them; and I knew I'd be toast if she found out! Two close friends at the school, who I knew would understand, had been the only ones I'd told about the worms, so I went to them and told them not to tell anyone! A couple of days later, at a staff meeting, somebody asked, "What was in those cookies?"

From the back of the room, in a very bitter voice, came, "It was worms!"

There were a number of gasps, quite a few snickers, and I did my best to slide under the table.

A couple of weeks later it was my birthday. It was the custom at the time for the birthday person to bring in a treat on their birthday (still doesn't make sense to me why we had to bring in our own treat, but that's another story). I had this great recipe for devil's food cake—from scratch—and I always made enough for a large and small cake. As expected, it was always gone by the end of the morning break. That year, however, at least two-thirds of it was still left at the end of the day. The next year, I tried again with the same results. After that, I just stopped at a favorite bakery and bought sweet rolls, as it was obvious my cooking was no longer appreciated.

Twelve years later, there was a note in all of our mailboxes and a little springy thing with a "worm" on it saying that Friday was "Worm Day" with the first graders. They were doing some worm activities related to a book they were reading and wanted all the staff to wear these little "worms." I thought, *Hmmm…it's been twelve years, but I wonder…* So on my way to school that day I stopped at a nice bakery and bought two dozen "gourmet oatmeal cookies" already pre-wrapped. I brought along a Tupperware container and simply wrote "Lee" on the side of it and dumped in the cookies. I set them in the lounge and said nothing. I then told my fifth graders the whole story about what I'd done twelve years before and told them I didn't know if they would remember or if they'd eat them. There had been some turnover. So many of the staff from twelve years ago weren't even around anymore. The kids promised to keep it a secret as long as I'd let them have any that might be leftover. At the end of the day, I went and checked and, much to the delight of my fifth graders, there were eighteen of the twenty-four cookies still left and my kids ate well. Don't ever believe it if anyone tells you that educators don't have good, or in this case, bad memories!

Chocolate Chip Worm Cookies

- Boil one or two night crawlers or two or three earthworms or three or four red worms. (If you keep the live worms in cornmeal for a few days before using them, they won't be quite so "gritty.")
- Fry them in butter, and then cut them up into small pieces.
- Mix the following together:
    - 1½ cups of presifted flour
    - 1½ cup of brown sugar
    - 1 teaspoon of baking soda
    - 1 teaspoon of salt
    - 1 cup of shortening (I actually prefer butter or a mixture of the two)
    - 2 eggs
    - 1 teaspoon of vanilla
    - 1 tablespoon of *hot* water
- Slowly stir in the following:
    - 2 cups of regular oatmeal (not the instant)
    - 1 package of chocolate (I prefer a *big* bag and *dark* chocolate)
    - 1 cup of walnut pieces
    - as many of the worm pieces as you dare
- Refrigerate the batter overnight before baking.
- Bake each batch at 375° for eight minutes.

Chapter 5
Sex Education

In our district during my teaching days, fifth grade is where we really got into the teaching of "Human Growth and Development" (sex education). They'd get a little bit in fourth grade, but got into the real nitty-gritty in fifth. I always felt kind of badly that my girls had to learn these things from a man teacher (although we did split the classes so the boys were with me and the girls with my female partner for a day when they covered the more personal things). I'd always begin my first class with all my fifth graders talking about various other systems of the human body. Among other things, I emphasized the importance of using correct terminology—using the correct names for each body part. I tell them, "When learning those systems, you won't hear me referring to the heart as the 'ticker,' the skull as your 'noggin,' or the stomach as the 'tummy' even though we would all know what I was talking about. I, therefore, will be calling a penis a penis and a vagina and vagina."

After the gasps, occasional fainting, and getting them all to crawl back out from underneath their desks, I move on with the lesson, "the ice having been broken!" One year, shortly after this speech, a little girl raised her hand with a question (this in itself was unusual as it normally takes quite some time before they can even look at me, say nothing about asking questions!) Anyway, her question, asked as innocently as could be, was, "Is a pecker the same as a penis? I've heard my dad use that word a lot but never knew what he was talking about until now." (I knew her dad well and could hardly wait for the right time to share that with him!)

The questions asked by these innocent youngsters (yes, despite what you may think, the great majority of ten- and eleven-year-olds are still very innocent) are incredible. For example, one boy said, "My older brother told me that red dye found in a lot of pop can stop your penis from growing. Is that true?" Although very tempted to confirm his concerns just to keep the kids from drinking so much pop, I did dispel the rumor.

One year, I had the other fifth-grade teacher's daughter in my class. She was a wonderful little girl but definitely put into a tough spot. During the initial introduction of the unit and the lecture on using the correct terminology of the human body parts, she turned her chair completely around to face the back wall, put her head in her hands, and just sat there shaking her head. She wasn't one to embarrass easily, but this was just too much for her. I, of course, got a chuckle and passed the reaction on to her mother. When her mom questioned her on it that evening, she simply said, "How would you expect me to react? I have to learn about sex from a man—and not just *any* man, but my mom's best friend, knowing that lots of my friends were right next door learning all of this from my mom! I had to turn around as there was no hole to crawl into!"

Any time we are in the out-of-doors, I make a point of teaching about various plants, especially edible wild foods. On our annual camping trip in September, I take them on the previously mentioned "nonnature hike." One of the plants I show them is yarrow, a very common plant that grows readily in disturbed areas such as our yards.

Yarrow

Native Americans used to make a rather bitter tasting tea out of it to use for stomachaches. In the spring, after the Human Growth and Development class, we will invariably come across yarrow while out hiking. I now "expand" their knowledge of the plant by being more specific—those stomachaches were often caused by menstrual cramps. One hike led to a child, not remembering the name yarrow, yelling to me, "Mr. Lee, here's one of those menstrual plants!" They had come a long ways from the initial embarrassment of hearing the correct terminology of that first Human Growth and Development class. They had maybe been a bit *too* desensitized? I also had some explaining to do, as I had several parent volunteers along on the hike who were likely wondering what the heck I was teaching their kids.

A coworker of mine, in an always entertaining lounge discussion during our sex education teaching times, told of her husband's "sex talk" with their young teenage son. He simply told him, "You have two heads—do your thinking with the big one!" Short, to the point, and likely quite effective!

Chapter 6
Table A

I've heard many times from educators that you need to be careful when in the teachers' lounge. It can be easy to get wrapped up in negativity and venting about the difficulty of our job. I even made that clear to both of my teacher children. My wife and I both often advise them, as well as our grandchildren, to "surround yourselves with positive people."

Now with that in mind, I never had that problem at Trempealeau Elementary. My time in the teachers' lounge was always the highlight of my days. It seemed like continuous laughter from the time we entered until the bell rang to tell us to get back to our classrooms.

As you walked in, there was a large table just inside the door and another toward the back of the lounge. The first people in, of course, settled into that first table, and the overflow sat at the back table. Table A, as it jokingly became known as, was always full and became the hub of the lounge. It almost became a race to get to Table A, and those that got there a little too late either crammed themselves into the table anyway or were "banished" to Table B. They then had to listen to the constant laughter and carrying on of Table A (from the distance of maybe six feet).

One never knew where the conversation would go at Table A. I was, quite often, the only male in the lounge. That never seemed to squelch the female-related topics. I kind of became one of the gals, I guess. I can't possibly tell all of the fun subjects discussed or this book would rival *War and Peace* in length. I can, however, give you a couple of samples.

There was the day where one of the teachers mentioned her recent mammogram. They all, of course, had to go into great detail of the process of squishing their breasts into some machine to get a picture and the discomfort involved. I just kind of sat back and

33

smiled as embarrassment was no longer an issue for me, although it probably should have been. They then decided that it wasn't fair and that maybe they should invent some kind of "penisgram" for men so we could see what it was like. Oh, how I hope that never happens!

Bath towels became the topic another day. Cindy insisted that she had to have a clean, fresh towel every time she showered. I, always the environmentalist, insisted that that was not a good idea. I then told them how I countered the fresh towel thing by always using the side of the towel with the label on it for the lower half of my body and the other side for the top half. Most thought that seemed like a pretty reasonable alternative for reasons I won't go in to. Cindy, however, still insisted she needed a fresh one every shower.

The next day with our regular Table A crew, one of the women staff made the comment, "I bet a lot of you, like me, thought of Scott when you took your shower last night." Oooo—wrong thing for her to say at Table A! She took a razzing for weeks after that about her "fantasies" of me while showering. She likely turned into a Cindy, requiring a clean, fresh towel every shower she took after that.

As mentioned earlier, the fifth grade teaching of Human Growth and Development led to many lively conversations. The rest of Table A looked forward to that week or two in the spring when it was being taught as the other fifth-grade teacher and I always had some entertaining stories of questions and comments made by our naïve eleven-year-old students.

I miss Table A! I know I can't go back to that, but it sure brings back great memories. I was so lucky to be surrounded by that group of positive people. There was never negative talk about our students, staff, administration, parents, or life in general. The teachers' lounge became the most positive, fun place in the entire school, far from the stereotypical place it often is portrayed.

34

Chapter 7
Night Hike

We took all the fifth and sixth graders on a two-day nature experience starting my second year of teaching, including camping overnight in tents at Perrot State Park. I thought it was an incredible experience for the kids, as it was often the first tenting opportunity of their lives and a hands-on experience with nature. (Evidently not all the other teachers shared my sentiments; however, they quit doing the overnight portion of the two days the year after I retired. I guess they didn't dare tell me that while I was still teaching.)

During the two days we did a variety of activities such as "Protective Coloration," "Wolf/Deer Scent Game," "Pit—Food Chain Game," the "Nonnature Hike" previously mentioned, and a couple of other hikes, including a night hike. Directions for these activities are included in the following pages. The night hike was my favorite, as we went into the "deep, dark woods" and gave them an opportunity to hike a stretch of it on their own. Although kind of scary for ten-year-olds, most of them did it themselves, and others were encouraged (but never forced, although peer pressure certainly helped give them the courage) to at least try it with a friend. I always had an adult stationed about halfway through the maybe one-hundred-yard stretch just in case one was needed, but they never were called upon to help. To be at the end waiting for them and seeing how excited they were to "make it" was wonderful for me. You'd think they had conquered Mount Everest.

Neither the kids nor the adults were ever allowed to take flashlights on my night hikes—that has always been an absolute "no-no." The main difference between a day hike and night hike is the light, so if everyone uses a flashlight, we might as well go during the day. I also emphasize that we can develop better night vision if we're in the dark for a while, but how easy it is to lose that night vision when a flashlight is turned on. I talk about the pupils in the eyes expanding when it's dark to allow any available light to get in to aid in their sight. To demonstrate that, I'd have the kids gather around an adult and focus on their eyes. I then have all the adults shine their flashlight into their own eyes when I say. It is always an "oooooo" and "ahhhhh" moment when they see how quickly the pupils shrink with all that available light. The night vision is gone in just seconds, but it will take ten to fifteen minutes of dark to get it back again. This seems to be enough to convince them to keep the flashlights off (although the poor adult guinea pigs tend to stumble around blindly for those next ten to fifteen minutes).

Nocturnal animals have specially designed eyes that give them better night vision. All animals' eyes, including ours, have both rods and cones in them. More rods give better night vision, while more cones assist in seeing color. Animals such as deer, who are more active at night, have more rods than we do, therefore, their ability to see in the dark much better than we can. They don't have as many cones; however, so their color vision isn't as good. They're not color blind but are limited as to which colors they can see. Deer can see blues and greens, for example, but not reds, yellows, and, most important to hunters, orange—especially blaze orange that is required for hunters during hunting season. I, therefore, carry a flashlight on these hikes that has a red light by putting red cellophane over it so the light is red and not visible to nocturnal animals.

One year, I decided to throw in a couple of surprises for the kids. I have access to a mounted skunk and owl, so with the help of a couple of staff friends, we were able to come across a "live" skunk and owl while hiking (fairly realistic puppets also work as the light from the red flashlight doesn't give them an opportunity to see them very clearly). The script for each is on the next pages, but basically we hear some rustling, and I spot the skunk off to the side. After getting real excited at our find, I explain that a skunk can only spray about twelve feet, so I'm going to try to get a little closer so we can see it better with my not-so-bright red flashlight. As I move in, the skunk suddenly warns, "I wouldn't get any closer if I were you." Showing the appropriate excitement of actually finding a skunk that can talk,

I ask her a variety of questions so we can all learn about skunks. Eventually, I ask her if she could come close so we could all touch her. She refuses, of course, but finally agrees to a compromise. Insisting that we all turn around, she "takes off her fur" and throws out her pelt (I have a real skunk pelt). Excitement again and I pass it around. She eventually tells us she's getting cold, so I pass the fur back to her after everyone again turns around. A few more questions for her after she "gets dressed," and then we hear an owl hoot back behind us. In fear, the skunk panics and disappears.

Striped Skunk
(Photo by Allen Blake Sheldon, Trempealeau)

I then decide to check out where the owl had hooted, and low and behold, there's a great horned owl sitting on a low branch. After the appropriate disbelief of how lucky we are to have another critter around, I go through the same process of trying to get closer and the owl telling us not to—yet another critter that talks and another first-hand opportunity to learn directly from the source. After a Q and A with him and learning all about owls, I ask about being able to touch him. He finally agrees to "take off his wing" for the kids to touch and later one of his talons (I have extra owl wings and talons). He eventually gets rather ornery with us as he was hoping to have that skunk for his late-night snack, and we have scared it off. He explains that due to a lack of the ability to smell, the skunk's defense mechanism doesn't work with him. His strong, sharp talons enable him to catch and kill it, and his beak is used to tear it apart. We then head out away from him and allow him to continue his hunt.

Owl Display at Trempealeau Elementary
Great gray, great horned, barred, long-eared, screech, saw-whet

I've done this activity with a number of groups, but found that it's not the best with fifth graders. Younger kids are in awe and believe it all and older kids and adults gladly go along with it. Ten- and eleven-year-olds, however, are too old to believe and too young to play along, so they tend to let me know that I can't fool them, and some recognize the skunk's or owl's voice. As a result, it wasn't a very successful try with them. I decided to try it again the next year with the same results. However, when I was all done with my planned tricks, I heard some rustling in the brush nearby; and all of a sudden, this large, hairy critter came charging out at me, growling and making quite a commotion. The kids and adult chaperones, of course, assumed it was just "part of the show," so had no fear at all, but I nearly had a heart attack (not to mention a near disaster in my pants). Turns out it was the father of one of my students with a coyote skin over his back charging on his hands and knees. I'd had his other daughter the year before, and he had been on that hike. He figured I might try it again, and he came prepared! My skunk and owl knew about it. My kids and other adults were entertained with the extension of the show, and I was nearly scared to death! That was my last time attempting this with my fifth graders; however, it continues to be a big hit with the little ones, older ones, and their parents.

Night Hike Directions—Skunk

Skunk's "Duties"

Have a "skunk" moving slightly as we approach—just enough to be noticed.

I'll make a big deal about being able to see a skunk and eventually say something about trying to get closer. I'll explain that a skunk can only spray accurately up to about twelve feet, so I'll be safe. I'll also tell them to watch its front feet, as they will stomp them up and down as a warning, and also have them listen for a hiss or growl. *Don't say anything until I've explained all that, and I start moving closer.* At that point, say something like, *"I wouldn't come any closer if I were you!"*

I'll get all excited about having a skunk that can talk, and then start asking you some questions:

- Why are you out at night? *(hunting for food, and that's when it's easiest and safest to find the food you like best)*
- What do you eat? *(insects, small rodents like mice, eggs, fruit)*
- What do you do all day? *(hide, sleep, rest)*
- Where do you live? *(underground dens)*
- How big do you get? *(one to one and a half feet and about five to ten pounds—and that you're full grown now)*

I'll say something about how neat it would be to be able to touch the skunk as there are a lot of people with me that have never touched a skunk before. Say *"no"* but when I insist, finally say, *"Okay, but you all have to turn around!"* I'll tell everyone to turn around, and then you "take off" your fur, and throw the pelt to me. I'll get all excited again about how you undressed for us, and I'll pass the pelt around for everyone to touch. After a bit, say, *"Brrrr…I'm getting cold! Please hurry!"* And I'll throw it back to you. Again, tell us to *"turn around"* so you can get dressed. You then reappear to chat some more.

I'll eventually ask about your enemies. Mention *people are your worst enemies due to trapping and getting hit by cars.*

I'll ask if they have any enemies besides people. Hopefully, the owl will then "hoot." You then get a panicky voice, and say you *have to leave right away!* You then disappear and say no more.

Skunk is done!

Mounted skunk from school display used for night hike

Night Hike Directions—Owl

Owl's "Duties"

When I ask the skunk if it has any other enemies besides people, you *"hoot."*

After skunk disappears, I'll focus my attention (red flashlight) toward the mounted owl. I'll then theorize as to why the skunk left in such a hurry and how neat it is to be so close to an owl.

When I say something about being real quiet and that I'll try sneaking a little closer, you say something like, *"That's close enough!"*

I'll then make a big deal about having another critter that talks and start asking some questions such as the following:

- How big do you get? *(about two feet but only about ten pounds and that you're now full grown)*
- Where do you live? *(prefer evergreen trees as they're better hiding places)*
- When and where do you nest? *(usually "borrow" crow or hawk nests or in holes in trees—on eggs by end of February and eggs hatch by end of March—two to four eggs)*
- What do you eat? *(rodents like mice, squirrels, rabbits, birds, and skunks. Get mad at us for scaring a potential meal away!)*

After you mention skunks, I'll question how you can stand killing and eating skunks. *(you have no sense of smell)*

I'll ask if you'd let us touch you. You say *"no!"* but when I insist, finally give in but tell us to *"turn around."* I'll get excited and have everyone turn around. You then throw out a wing. I'll pass it around and let everyone touch it. When I give it back, again tell us to *"turn around."*

I'll then ask about your feet/talons. Again, *eventually agree if we turn around,* and throw out a talon after I tell everyone to turn around. I'll pass it around, and when I return it, have everyone turn around again.

You can then tell us to *please leave as you are getting hungry and have to find something to eat.* We'll thank you and leave.
Owl is done!

Great horned owl from school display case used for night hike

Wolf/Deer Scent Game

Age Group/Size:
- All ages and sizes will work, but twenty to twenty-five people is ideal.

Setting:
- Outside, preferably a wooded area or long-grass prairie.

Materials:
- Sponges cut into small pieces (about fifty pieces per "pack")
- Various scents (clear vanilla, lemon, perfume, anise, etc.)
- Two ziplock sandwich bags per pack
- Blanket or poncho for each deer

Directions:

Divide group into wolf packs (Three packs of about six to eight is ideal, but more packs is all right, minimum of two packs). One person from each pack must be a deer. Each pack and their deer will be assigned a scent and given the bag of sponge pieces soaked in that scent. With the "wolves" not watching, each of the "deer," with their own scented bag of sponges, will wander through the designated area, dropping one of their sponges every three steps. The deer may cross each other's paths, double back, wind back and forth, etc. to leave a confusing trail that the wolves will be attempting to follow. When they start running out of sponges, they must find a good hiding place. They can use the blanket or poncho to lie on to hide as well as possible—they may be there for a while!

While the deer are laying out their scent trail, each pack of wolves needs to come up with their own special "howl" (such as one long howl or a series of "yips" or three short howls, etc.). This will be their only form of communication once the "hunt" begins, so they must be able to recognize the other members of their own pack by that howl.

Grey wolf and whitetail deer
(Forty miles north of Trempealeau and
Perrot State Park in Trempealeau)

When the deer have their scent trails out and are hidden, the wolves are taken to the starting point and begin the hunt. Whenever they find a sponge, they pick it up and smell it. If it is *not* their scent, they must replace it where they found it. If it is theirs, they need to alert the rest of their pack by using their special howl and put the sponge into their bag. The rest of the pack then comes to assist in searching that area. They should know that another sponge should be within three steps of that spot. They only howl when they find their scent and can use no other language to communicate.

The hunt continues until each of the wolf packs finds their own deer. If they accidently find another deer, they should not let the other packs know—just continue to search for their own deer.

Pit

(Food Chain Game)

Where to play:
- An outside location is best as it involves some running and yelling, but it could be played in a classroom or gym with some restrictions.

Materials:
- Index cards (sixty), whistles (one for each group of about six)

Preparation:
- Come up with a food chain of ten things, such as sun, grass, grasshopper, spider, praying mantis, frog, snake, raccoon, wolf, and Turkey vulture.
- Make six cards of each of the ten on the index cards—a total of sixty cards (laminating them would be wise if you plan to continue to use the game as they get rather rough treatment).

Directions:
- Divide group into about four or five groups, and give each group a whistle (whistle isn't necessary, they can just yell when they get done).
- Mix up and deal out the cards among the groups. Each group must have at least ten to twelve cards.
- When told to begin, have each group organize their cards, and attempt to form a food chain with them. Tell them there are ten different things in the food chain, so if they are missing some, they must trade with other groups to get what they need as in the real "pit" game.

Object of the Game:
- Collect at least one of each object in the food chain—ten items in all

Trading Rules:
- All trading must take place in a designated area (such as by a tree centered among the groups) by only one person in the group (a different person may go after each trade, however).
- Trader must trade all the same kind with each trade (three grass or two wolves) by yelling the number of items they wish to trade (yell "Three, three, three!" or "Two, two, two!").
- Trader should not show others what they're trying to trade.
- After a trade is made, trader must return to his/her group. The group then must decide what items are still needed and which can still be traded in order to complete their food chain. If the food chain is not completed, another person from the group must go and trade.
- Continue making trades in this way until the group has determined that they have at least one of each item in the food chain. When they get the chain in the correct order, they immediately let you know (by blowing their whistle or yelling).
- The first group with all ten items and in the correct order is the winner. They will likely want to play it more than once.

Chapter 8
Protective Coloration

One year, the sixth graders, for an art project before Christmas, were assigned in pairs to decorate the doors of each room in the school. The two who were to do my door put up white paper right away but never seemed to get back to do any decorating. After a few days with a plain, white door, I decided to "help them out" a bit. On the door, I put up a sign saying, "This beautiful artwork created by (Debbie and Steve) very creatively shows the concept of 'Protective Coloration.' The trained eye will be able to find the following wildlife":

- arctic fox, snowshoe hare, snowy owl, ermine, snow bunting, seagull
- white ibis, whooping crane, arctic tern, tundra swan, polar bear, ptarmigan
- cattle egret, white pelican, snow goose, bald eagle (head only), albino whitetail deer

I don't think they ever did put any Christmas decorations on the door, as they were getting lots of compliments on their "artwork." What was amazing is how many kids came up to me and said they'd found every one of the critters—and many were serious!

I never did care for having to do bulletin boards, and it seemed that every classroom I ever occupied in my career had way too many of them. I, therefore, expanded that Christmas doorway idea and turned them into seasonal bulletin boards. I used a similar sign reading: "This beautiful limited addition of a winter scene, 'Winter Camouflage,' is the second in a series of paintings called 'The Four Seasons.' This is printed, numbered, and signed by Scott Lee very 'creativelee' demonstrates the concept of Protective Coloration. The trained eye will be able to find the following wildlife."

The first day of each season, I'd take down one color of paper and put up another. Autumn was brown with critters like whitetail deer (lying down), brown snake, walking stick, American toad, winter wren, river otter, wood frog, brown salamander, moth, brown bear, mosquito, and veery. Spring was green with smooth green snake, monk parakeet, barking treefrog, female painted bunting, luna moth, katydid, green anole, green lizard, inchworm, chameleon, and green stink bug. I didn't have to do summer, but did have a group of blue critters on hand, just in case, such as the male mountain bluebird, indigo bunting, etc.

I even framed the series and gave them away as Christmas gifts a couple of times. I had given a signed and numbered set of all four in the series one Christmas but was disappointed when I'd visited her house and they weren't prominently displayed on her living room walls. She eventually returned them, assuming, I guess, I could regift them, but how can one regift something so valuable?

A good activity to demonstrate the concept of "Protective Coloration" is on the following pages.

Protective Coloration Activity

Why are green insects green? Why are brown insects brown? The answers can be complicated, but this activity will help explain.

Directions:

Get five colors of yarn (forest green, brown, red, white, and yellow), and cut it into about one to two-inch lengths. For a class of twenty-five, you should have equal numbers of about one hundred of each color (the more you have of each, the better the results). At game time, have the students scatter the yarn pieces in a selected outdoor area (you can do this yourself ahead of time, but I've found that the kids don't always believe that there are equal numbers of each color when they're done collecting them, so it's better to have them spread them out). A grassy field such as a lawn works great, but you could do it in a wooded area or even on the snow in winter. The area should be at least 50 X 50 as a smaller area makes it too easy.

Start talking to the group about birds and their food choices. When insects are mentioned, discuss the main sense a bird would use to try to find insects. They must *see* it first (in fact, many birds have no sense of smell at all). Explain that they will be "hungry birds" and that the "insects" they need to survive are the yarn pieces they just scattered. They must hunt for them by using their sense of sight (they can walk, run, crawl, whatever, but will soon find out that walking is their best strategy). Upon "release" of the birds on their hunt, watch to see how successful they seem to be—you *don't* want them to find them all, so two to five minutes will likely be enough time.

After calling time, have them congregate in an area (picnic table?) where they can separate the yarn by color and count each color or have five students collect all of each color and total them up.

Discussion:

Get the totals of each, and discuss the results (in a normal grassy area, they will most likely find most of the red and white, fewer of the yellow, very few greens, and hardly any browns). Was one color found more than others? (probably the red) Was one found less than others (brown or green)? What does this information tell us about survival of various colored insects? What might be the results if we spread the yarn pieces in a real grassy area? In the snow? Under some trees in late fall?

Ask students if it would be accurate to say, "The insects living on green plants are green so that people or predators can't see them." This is *not* an accurate statement because it implies that insects can determine what color they want to be. It would be more correct to say, "Most insects that are found on green plants are green insects because these are the ones that predators cannot see as easily and haven't eaten them." Point out that insects come in a variety of colors. Over centuries of evolution, through a process of natural selection, those that were eaten by predators were those that did not blend in with their background unless they developed another defense mechanism. Green insects have tended to survive best on green plants, brown insects against a brown background, etc. If time allows, you can send them back out to try to find all the ones they missed, especially the browns and greens.

Examples of exceptions to the rules of protective coloration:

- bees (yellow and black is *the most* visible color combination there is, therefore, school bus colors, but bees have stingers)
- ladybugs (part of the hard-shelled beetle family, which makes them difficult to eat)
- monarch butterflies (main food as a caterpillar is milkweed, which is toxic to most other critters—makes the monarchs taste bad)
- viceroy butterfly (uses "mimicry" by imitating the coloration of the bad-tasting monarch)

Chapter 9
A Pet Snake?

I attended many environmental education conferences around Wisconsin and the Midwest. As a fundraiser, they would often have a silent auction on items nature-related that members of the various organizations would donate. Because it was a fundraiser for very worthy organizations, people would normally bid way too high for things, knowing it was going to a good cause. One year at the Midwestern Environmental Education Conference in St. Paul, one of the items was a baby boa constrictor only three months old. The mother lived in a nature center in Ames, Iowa, and I had been there the year before when I was down to the previous Midwest Environmental Education Conference, so had "met" her. She had given birth to forty baby boas, so they donated one to be auctioned off at the St. Paul conference. It was three months old and only about eighteen inches, and they were asking a minimum bid of $40. The conference went until Sunday afternoon, and on Saturday evening, someone had bid $25 and another bid $28. I was not a fan of snakes at all. It wasn't a phobia-type fear, but I definitely was not comfortable holding them. I thought it would make for a good story to come back to school and tell my staff friends (who knew I wasn't a snake fan) that I'd actually bid on this snake, so I decided to put in a bid for $30. Little did I know that the bidding was going to close five minutes later, and I would be announced as the winner, and now the proud father of this bouncing baby boa. I thought the bidding went until Sunday, and with a minimum asking bid of $40, there was no chance of me "winning!" Needless to say, my thoughts were flawed!

After getting past the initial panic, I started thinking this through. I knew my wife would not let me keep it at our house, as she was worse than me with her fear. I had no idea if the school would allow me to have it in my room. I then had to figure out how

SPIDERS AND SNAKES AND RATS—OH MY!

to get it home as the cage wasn't included in the bidding price. My only option, it seemed to me, was to "borrow" the pillowcase off the bed from my motel room (I did leave a nice tip for the maid to rid myself of a little guilt) and have the snake ride back home next to me in my pickup seat, so one problem solved.

Now I had to face my wife and kids. My kids (daughter, ten and son, six) were always very happy to see me come home from these conferences. It might have something to do with the fact that I would always bring them a little something, but I want to think it was only because they missed me so much. Anyway, when I arrived home, they all greeted me with open arms and, as usual, the first words out of the kids' mouths were, "Did you get us anything?"

I replied, "Oh, yes—I got you something *really* special this time!"

They asked what it was, and I repeated, "It's *really* special!"

This got my wife's attention, and she said (knowing me too well, I think), "If it breathes, I'm leaving!"

I moved toward her for a hug, and she, backing away, repeated, "I mean it—if it breathes, I'm leaving!"

That problem was definitely *not* solved.

We headed out to the garage and my truck—kids, excited; wife, not so much. I reached into the pillowcase on my front seat and pulled out the snake. My daughter screamed and ran for the house, my son jumped high off the ground, and my wife just glared. She informed me, very matter-of-factly, that, "that thing is not coming in this house!" I told her that I was taking it to school in the morning.

She said, "No, it is *not* coming in this house!"

I tried once more to emphasize that I'd take it to school in the morning (still not sure how problem #3 was going to go), but it was clear that I'd be taking the seventeen-mile trip to school to drop it off on that Sunday night.

I grabbed the newspaper, checked the want ads, and luckily found a ten-gallon aquarium for sale about five miles from the house and headed out there to buy it. I then made the drive to drop the snake off at school, hoping that that problem would have a better solution. Luckily my principal, unbeknownst to me, had previously owned a snake and was a big fan. He had no problem letting me keep it in my room. The rest of the staff was not feeling quite so welcoming; however, Boaregard managed to spend the last twenty-two years of my career in my fifth-grade classroom and died a year and a half later in one of the first grade classrooms at the age of twenty-three and a half. He was, by far, the best $30 I ever spent for educational props, as he helped educate thousands of kids of all ages. In those twenty-two years with my fifth graders, there were only two students that did not hold him, and I can honestly say that not one of my students grew up with anything that would even resemble a phobia of snakes.

Chapter 10
Boaregard

Boaregard, my boa constrictor, was a wonderful classroom pet. He was very low-maintenance, only eating about once a month, and therefore, only messing the cage with that same frequency. Every time we held him, he would wrap around you in a big hug. He never made any noise to interrupt class. He was just plain easy compared to the many other pets I'd had in my room along the way—guinea pigs, lop-eared rabbits, turtles, frogs, iguana, rats, mice, hamster, and a couple other snakes.

Boaregard and three fifth-grade fans

There were some memorable moments with him, however. He was generally good, but did manage to bite four times. His first victim was Jody, one of my fifth graders. When he was little and still in the ten-gallon aquarium, I would allow my students to get him out as long as I was there, and they had my permission. One girl, who was one of the shortest in my class, was trying to get him out by herself, but he wrapped his tale around the edge of the cage, and she couldn't reach high enough to get him out. Rather than slide her lower hand down to get his tail free, she let go of his head. The snake, in panic, started flopping round, so Jody, a taller girl and also Boaregard's "best friend" that year, jumped to the rescue. Unfortunately the snake reacted to the incoming hand and bit her. No harm done, didn't even break the skin, but the speed with which a snake strikes is enough to scare anyone, even his best friend Jody. Jody handled it extremely well and remained his best friend. I knew her parents very well, so called them to let them know what had happened. They were more concerned that it may cause Jody to be scared of the snake than whether or not she got hurt, as she had talked about the snake a lot, and they knew she loved him.

A few years later, I got a new student in my room. He was a great kid but had had some issues in his other school, so the thought was that he might do better with a male teacher. He was fascinated with the snake, so I got him out and let John hold him and show him to the new boy. John was Boaregard's best friend that year and was very good handling him. I was right there but turned my back for a bit, and all of a sudden several of the kids yelled. I turned around, and Boaregard had bit John on his upper arm. His teeth didn't even go through to the skin, but they got stuck in John's sleeve and couldn't shake them out. I quickly grabbed the snake, untangled his teeth from John's shirt, and put him back in the cage. I could not figure out why he'd bitten until after school when one of the boys stuck around to talk to me. He said the new boy had jabbed the snake with a pencil, and the snake, in pain and having no other way to communicate that, bit who was holding him, his best friend, John. The new boy had a great year, and I had no other problems with him. He also loved Boaregard and handled him a lot. John's mom, like Jody's, felt badly only because she was afraid John might become afraid of the snake as he too had talked a lot about how much he loved Boaregard. He didn't seem phased and continued through the year as Boa's best friend.

The snake also bit me a couple of times, both of which were my fault. The first was during his first summer when I'd gone in to feed him. He hadn't been handled for about a month, and I reached in too quickly to pick him up. I'm sure I scared him, and he let me know in the only way he could. I had one tiny puncture on my hand with a little bead of blood. It scared me, and for the rest of the summer, I wore long-sleeved shirts and gloves every time I picked him up. That was the summer of 1988, one of the hottest summers on record, but I still kept the long sleeves and gloves on.

The last time he bit me was when he was much bigger—over nine feet—and again, it was a real boneheaded mistake by me. It was one of the first weeks of school, and the first time I would be feeding him in front of my fifth graders (and also a student teacher). He lived in a large cage with a glass front. He was eating pretty large rats by then that I would thaw out. Snakes sense food by heat picked up by their tongue. All the kids were sitting close to the glass front, so I explained to them that as soon as he sensed the right heat and that it was the right size (both determined by their tongue as they have rather poor eyesight), he would strike at the first thing that moved. I, therefore, told them that once I open the top of the cage with the rat, they could not move at all, or he would strike toward them and bang his poor nose on the glass. Just before I opened the cage, one of the kids asked why his eyes were a bluish-gray color when they normally were brown. Not all the kids could see that, so I set the rat down on top of the cage and, like a dummy, picked up the snake and pulled him out. I had intended to explain to them that when snakes are getting ready to shed, they will grow a layer of skin over their eyes so when the dead skin peels off, it won't hurt their eyes. Before I could finish explaining that, however, the snake sensed the rat that I'd set right on the cage where I'd pulled him out. To prove to the kids that I knew what I was talking about (and also prove that my short-term memory needs some work), the snake struck at the first thing that moved, just as I'd said. Unfortunately, that was my hand!

This time was different than his previous strikes, however. This time was not in fear and sending out a warning. This time he thought he was grabbing food, so he hung on! The wide-eyed kids nearly panicked. I did a pretty good job of hiding my fear and explained that he would eventually realize that my hand and arm are not food—or at least that I'm too big to swallow—and let go. In the meantime, the blood was starting to cover my hand from the many teeth that were stuck in it. I really wasn't in pain, as boa constrictors' teeth are quite small as they only use them for hanging on, not for killing. In what seemed to be hours, but in reality was likely only five to seven minutes, he finally worked his teeth loose. I quickly threw him in the cage and dropped the rat in after him. Normally, I hold it by the tail and move it around as he's looking for movement, and he grabs it out of my hand. I wasn't taking any more chances this time—I'd had enough! When I washed the blood off my hand, we could hardly see the tiny puncture marks. I've been bit by lots of different critters (mice, gerbil, iguana, dogs, cats, etc.), but the snake bite was by far the least painful. It was, however, the scariest of the bites, as they are just so incredibly fast when they strike. My student teacher, in only her second week, told me later that she was getting very panicky, as she was afraid that I was going to ask her to come and pull the snake off my hand. I'm sure she was thinking, *How the heck am I going to survive another three months with this guy? Get me out of here!*

Boaregard in fifth-grade room with a fan

Chapter 11
Snake Escape!

The family of one of my students had a young boa constrictor, but really didn't want it anymore. They asked me if I'd be interested. Through the years of doing programs with Boaregard, including numerous teacher programs, I'd had many teachers express interest in having a snake as a classroom pet. I, therefore, thought there might be a "market" for baby snakes, so took the family up on the offer. I felt I could have Boaregard mate with "Connie" and supply these teachers, and maybe even make a little money in the process. I realized that Connie was a bit too small when I got her, so would have to postpone my plans for a few years (poor Boaregard was so disappointed, as he was "ready for romance!").

The eighth grade science teacher in a connecting building happily agreed to keep Connie in his room. In early August of the summer of 2001, I traded cages with his snake in order to take my snake to do a weeklong teacher academy I was teaching. When I returned, I switched the snakes around into their own cages but evidently didn't get the cover of Connie's cage on correctly. The next day I got a call from Al, the science teacher, asking me where Connie was, as he had come in to feed her. Knowing Al, I assumed he was just joking with me but soon found out the snake had escaped. With only a couple of weeks left before school starting, we knew the pressure was on to find her. The eighth grade part of the complex was the old Trempealeau High School—and I mean *real* old. We spent every night (boa constrictors are nocturnal) scouring that school looking for Connie. I found myself crawling through small, dark areas the likes of which I never want to go again. I knew she had to be getting hungry, so got a small cage and a live mouse as bait to draw her out. I'd move it around every night, putting powder around the cage so I could tell if she had crawled near the cage.

Nothing worked, and the first day of school arrived with Connie still on the loose. I knew any kind of popularity I may have had with my staff was in great jeopardy. I also knew that the junior high principal and custodian over there were both afraid of snakes, not to mention numerous other staff members. I was a wreck knowing I'd have to inform everyone of the situation, but knew it had to be done.

This was the fall of the tragedy of nine-eleven. On nine-twelve, some high school kids thought it might be fun to call in a bomb threat to the entire district. (Actually, he and his girlfriend in a nearby community wanted to spend the day together, so decided that a bomb scare would get school canceled and the day would be theirs. It worked for our district, but the other district already had a plan in place, and she only missed an hour of class. Their little romance went through some major disciplinary action and may have ended the relationship.) In our schools, the local police and fire departments were called in after all the kids were sent home. As a thorough search was going to be done, we asked the searchers to be on the lookout for the snake while they searched for the bomb. I was told that one of the county police officers, with an obvious fear of snakes, had his gun drawn for his entire search. I'm pretty sure he was much more concerned about the snake than any old bomb!

Well, to make a long story short, Connie has, to this day, never been seen or "heard" from since. Most of the staff had a good sense of humor over the whole thing but a couple still haven't forgiven me for the stress I caused. My greatest fear was that when I was well into my retirement years, I'd get a call saying, "Scott, would you please come in as we have a fourteen-foot boa constrictor wrapped around one of our students, and we'd like you to get her off!" Sixteen years after Connie's escape, that section of the complex was demolished and replaced by new construction, so I think I'm safe! My guess is that she somehow got outside soon after her escape but, being a tropical animal, would not have been able to survive even the cooler summer nights and definitely not the autumn or winter.

Chapter 12
Rats!

I got a call one day from a teacher acquaintance from another school saying she had two white rats that she no longer wanted to keep in her room. She had done some science experiments with them but was done, so she wondered if I wanted them. Boaregard was big enough to eat full-size rats by then, so I thought that would be great, as it would save me some money on snake food. She brought them over to me after school in nice cages and proceeded to tell me all about them—their names, what they liked to eat, about their personalities, etc. It quickly became very obvious that she wasn't bringing them over as "snake food" and that she would be horrified if she knew that that had been my intentions in accepting her offer. I, therefore, ended up with two more, and this time unintended, classroom pets.

The rats turned out to be wonderful additions to my room. They were so friendly, and the kids would get them out to play with as often as I'd let them. They'd crawl on the kids' shoulders and heads, were never aggressive at all, or made any attempt to escape. We all loved them, but had to be very careful not to get them too close to Boaregard's cage. He also would have loved them, but in a much different way. It was very sad for all of us when they each developed what I think were cancerous growths, became quite sick, and died within just a couple weeks of each other.

Two grandkids and their favorite "rat"

Chapter 13
Willow

I've done well over one hundred programs for various groups with snakes. Boaregard died on Christmas Day in 2009 at the age of twenty-three and a half years old and nine and a half feet long, but my son, after growing up with him, had developed a love for snakes. When he got done with college, he bought a little ball python of his own. Since Boaregard died, I have used Willow, his snake, to do programs. (He chose the name Willow for "her," but years later I pointed out that "she" was a "he"—much too late to change his/her name.) Willow has never even made an attempt to bite in his seventeen-plus years of life. He's full-grown at about four and a half feet and extremely mild-mannered.

That goes a long ways toward, but does not guarantee, a problem-free program. On two occasions, "nature called" for the snake during a program. If you've never experienced the smell from snake urine or bowel movement, consider yourself lucky! It is pretty disgusting. The last time was in church, as I was doing a program for Summer Bible School for the three local churches. I had about fifty elementary kids and was right toward the end, doing a rewrite of an MC Hammer rap called "Pray." I had changed the words to go along with a program I do on predators and prey (*See* words attached) and use the music from his rap as background. Anyway, I had spent thirty to forty minutes teaching them about several animals, including snakes, that people don't usually like (wolves, skunks, etc.). All of a sudden, there was a collective gasp, and a second or two later, my entire chest and stomach felt very wet and warm. Besides the urine all over me, the solid stuff was on my shoe and the floor. Needless to say, I lost the kids, and I'm sure the only thing they remember about the entire program was "Mr. Lee getting peed and pooped on." Judging by the many parents that teased me about it, that's also likely the only story that got home.

As if that wasn't enough for the evening, I then had to pack up everything and head down to one of the other churches to do the same program with about a dozen kindergarteners. I, of course, had no change of clothes, so had to put up with my smelly self the rest of the evening. Understandably, I didn't get any hugs from the kids when I got done, and that's always one of my favorite parts of working with these munchkins. Believe it or not, I was invited back that fall to do the same program to include all the kids, including those that had not been able to attend the summer Bible school. Willow behaved much better, and the kids might actually have learned something about snakes besides that they "pee and poop."

Willow and grandson Aiden

"Prey"

(Written by Scott Lee—1991)

We prey—that's right, we prey.
We need to prey just to make it today,
And so we prey—we've *got* to prey!
If we don't prey, we'll be hungry all day!

(Chorus)

All us *snakes*—you people hassle, treat us bad,
Say we're slimy—mean and ugly—makes us sad ☹
You think we're wrong to eat cute critters every day,
But if we don't, we will die—and so we prey!

(Chorus)

In all those tales 'bout us *wolves*—we don't look good!
They say we eat those little pigs—*and Riding Hood!*
We don't eat people—that's not true what they say,
We mind our business, raise our pups—and also prey!

(Chorus)

Silent wings plus eyes and ears that can't be beat,
Beak for tearing—strong, sharp talons on our feet.
We're not so dumb—we hunt at night and *hide* all day.
Mice and squirrels (even *skunks!*)—on that we prey!

(Chorus)

You all hate us—say we stink (I guess that's true),
But try to kill us—even hurt us—you'll get what's due!

Don't get close or think that you'll make *us* your prey,
'Cause if you do, we'll have no choice except to *spray*!

(Chorus)

Oh, yes, we spray—that's right, we spray.
If we don't spray, we might end up your prey,
And so we spray—we've *got* to spray!
We've got to spray just to make it today!

(Chorus)

Time and time and time and time and time again,
You people hurt us—even kill us—it's a sin!
You eat your burgers, steak, and ham—think *that's okay*,
But those were cows and pigs and so…*you* also prey!

(Chorus)

That's right, *you* prey—Oh yes, you prey,
You too must prey just to make it today,
But that's *okay* for you to prey,
Just don't condemn us when it's *us* who need to prey!

Chapter 14
Floppy

One school year I got a lop-eared rabbit for a room pet that the kids named "Floppy." I got him litter-box trained, so he was free to hop around the room all day. He was such an incredible addition to the room. Rather than being the distraction I'd feared he might be, he actually had a calming effect on the kids. Real often I'd see a student sitting quietly reading or whatever with Floppy sitting on their lap. The kids loved him!

He was not quite so nice to me, however. I don't know if I was a perceived threat to his masculinity or male competition or what, but at some point nearly every day, he would hop up to me, kick out his leg, and urinate all over my pants' leg. Every pair of pants I owned that year ended up with urine stains up and down my lower leg—a problem, that didn't exactly endear him to me (actually, I loved the little guy despite that irritating habit, as he often ended up hopping onto my lap as well).

He too became a pretty good escape artist as quite often the door would not get closed, and Floppy would take advantage. At least weekly, someone (usually the librarian across the hall or a sixth grader in the room next door) would come walking in, rabbit in hand to return him.

The following year I decided to create a home for the rabbit in a courtyard just outside my room, with only a single door to access the area. All the kids in the school had learned to love Floppy, so this became a great place for him to live where the entire school could visit and enjoy him. Seven different classrooms had windows out to the courtyard, so it was pretty rare that there weren't a number of kids with their noses pressed against the window keeping an eye on him.

My fifth graders were especially frequent visitors, stopping for a short visit each day on their way out to recess. One of my fifth-grade girls, who was especially fond of him, visited him every chance she had. One day, she came in to tell me just how much she liked Floppy and said, "I can tell he really likes me as well, as he always jumps up against me and 'hugs' me, rocking back and forth against my leg. I had to push him off today, though, as he 'peed' on my leg while 'hugging' it!" All I could think of was, *Oh, sweetheart, you are going to be so devastated come spring when we do our Human Growth and Development* [sex education], *and you realize just what he was really doing on your leg!*

Chapter 15
And They Keep on Escaping!

Connie, the boa constrictor, wasn't my only critter to escape in my career. When Boaregard was young, I'd catch live mice and feed them to the snake. Several times I had mice escape but managed, with the help of my fifth graders, to chase them down before getting out of my room.

My most memorable escapee was Charlotte, the tarantula (yeah, I know what you're thinking, *Really? You had a tarantula as a pet in a room full of ten-year-olds? What is wrong with you?*). She was actually a great pet. Like the snake, she was very low-maintenance—just drop in a few crickets every week or two, and put in new woodchips every month or so. Tarantulas don't deserve the bad reputation they have. They are very unaggressive, and if it would bite (which she never did in the seven or eight years I had her), it is far from deadly—comparable only to a bee sting. I got her out often and held her with my bare hands. I didn't let the kids hold her, but they would pet her often and loved having her around.

Tarantula

One Monday morning, I came in to find her cage empty! Yikes—a *big* problem! I rounded up Tom and Jane, two staff members who always liked Charlotte, to assist in the search. We had no luck, and then the kids arrived. They had no fear of her, so took over the search. Now my room was loaded with hiding places—lots of animal pelts, skulls, and many other nature-related items. Those kids searched the room, sticking their little hands in, around, and under everything—not sure that even I wanted to do that, but they checked everywhere!

Charlotte was gone, and once again, I had to face the staff with another lost critter. This principal was not happy and announced over the intercom, "Attention! Attention! Mr. Lee's tarantula has escaped and may be anywhere in the school. Do not get near it, and if you see it, immediately let us know!" You'd have thought it was a thousand-pound grizzly wandering around the school. I had to do what I could to quell the fear, so spent every free minute of the day going from room to room, talking to every classroom about tarantulas, and to simply let me know if they saw her. This escape was especially hard for me, as I knew one of my very best friends, the kindergarten teacher, had a severe case of arachnophobia. She had to go past my room on her way to most everywhere, so spent the next three weeks creeping past my room in tears and, of course, never set foot in my room. She continually apologized to me for her fear, but a phobia is a phobia, and she couldn't help it. (By the way, she is still one of my best friends so we survived it.)

The kids knew that I felt bad after losing Charlotte, and they also really missed her. Secretly they took up a collection and talked one of the mothers into making a trip to the nearest pet store to buy me a new tarantula as a gift. He (male tarantulas are smaller than females) was christened "Charlie" and moved into Charlotte's home. He didn't feel quite as safe as Charlotte, but we were learning to love him.

Not too long after Charlie's arrival and three and a half weeks after Charlotte's escape, over the intercom came a rather sudden plea from our secretary, "Scott, get down to the office right away!"

This was right at the end of the day, and the kids were just getting ready to go home, so about half my class followed me down there. In the office, we saw several people, including the UPS man, gathered around Charlotte. The UPS guy evidently saw it on the floor and laughingly started to pick it up, thinking it was a gag. Charlotte got into her defensive position (shackles up), so the UPS man realized it was real and raised his foot to step on her. Karen, the secretary, thankfully, stopped him and notified me. I simply put my hand down and coaxed her onto it for a ride back to my room to join Charlie in the cage.

Not really wanting a second tarantula, I tried to figure out where to find another cage and just what to do with them both. That solution came the next day with a scream from several kids. In the cage a "war of tarantulas" was taking place—Charlotte was attacking Charlie in a brutal fight. The question now became, "How do you break up a tarantula fight?" I opted for a ruler rather than my hand to break them up. I then removed Charlie and found temporary alternate housing. Sadly, he was dead by the end of the day—not exactly the way I wanted my problem solved. My girls were proud of Charlotte, and I'm guessing my boys were glad they weren't tarantulas!

Years later, a friend of my daughter's was heading off to college, so was looking for a home for her tarantula, *araña* (Spanish for spider). She came to me, and I agreed to give her a home, where she lived the rest of her life—maybe four or five years? Jane (a second-grade teacher who had been in the original search party for Charlotte) willingly agreed to take Charlotte, and she lived very happily with her and her second graders for many more years before passing on to that spidery heaven way up among the webs.

She also managed to escape from Jane's cage one time and was found a day later down at the end of the hall inside...wait for it... *Cheri's* room! My arachnophobic friend! Oh, the irony! Luckily, she didn't know about the escape, and it took Jane and I weeks before we dared to tell her how close she came to what would have likely been a major heart attack.

Chapter 16
The "A" Word

One day, while sitting at my desk, my fifth-grade teaching partner, came into my room. She marched back and stood in front of my desk and said, "Umm …umm…Darn it, I can't remember what I came in here to tell you! Geez, I hate when that happens. I must be getting… umm…umm."

I knew what she was trying to think of, knew it was a long "A" word, but also could not think of the word, so I said, "Anorexia."

She replied, "Yeah, anorexia. I must be getting anorexia!"

She then turned and left my room with me just staring at her with a smile on my face. I wondered how long before she realized she did not have "anorexia" but was thinking of that other long "A" word. I could almost hear her come to a screeching halt halfway back to her room, and she came back to my doorway saying, "IT'S NOT ANOREXIA!"

I told her that I knew that, but also couldn't think of that other long "A" word.

Through our remaining years together, we had many bouts of "anorexia" but are surviving it quite well.

Chapter 17
Mole Trolling

Very often while hiking, I come across a path of ground that is pushed up from underneath. If you have a lawn, you're probably familiar with your lawn mower's worst enemy—the lowly mole. When hiking with groups, I usually carry a mounted mole hidden in my pocket. Upon coming across one of these mole trails, we stop and I explain what caused it. I tell them what they eat (grubs, worms, roots, etc.) and that they spend their entire lives crawling around underground most of their time, searching for a good meal. They have huge front feet for digging and very rarely see the light of day.

I then go into a fictional report on how, if you stick your finger through the ground and into their tunnel and wiggle it around, they sometimes mistake it for a grub or worm and grab hold of it. I call it "mole trolling," and then demonstrate how it's done. I do tell them that it doesn't work very often, but once in a while I get lucky. After a bit, I indicate that I'm getting a "nibble." Their attention, of course, is on my finger in the ground, so I sneakily pull a mole mount I have hidden in my pocket. In a frenzy, I dig up the dirt while bringing the mount into the mess as if I just pulled him out of the ground. With a little wiggling around of the mount in my hand, they are all amazed that my "trolling" was a success. I keep them in awe with my exceptional mole-trolling abilities before finally showing that it's only a mount. I then pass it around so they can say they handled a real mole, albeit real dead.

Mole mount used for "mole trolling"
(Part of thirty-foot display case at Trempealeau Elementary School)

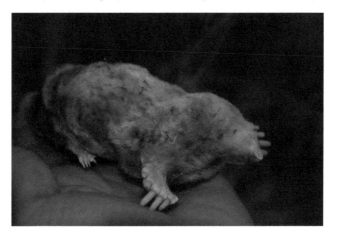

Chapter 18
Deer Dissection

In my mind, the most educational activity I ever did with the fifth graders was dissecting a whitetail deer. There are a number of ways I've heard to describe this activity—"gross," "yuch," "sick," "What is wrong with you?" are just a few—but nobody could argue the educational value of it. I've included the lesson plan on the following pages, but there are some basic things one needs to know to tackle this dissection.

1. When: I always did this in the winter as I needed to keep the road-killed deer buried in a snow bank to keep it from starting to decompose while not letting it freeze solid. It's gross enough without also having to deal with the odors of decomposition. The insulation of snow keeps it in perfect dissection condition.

2. Getting the deer: Depending on when winter decides to arrive around here, I contact the county and local police and have them keep an eye out for a road-killed deer that still seems to be in decent shape (in a dead sort of way). When they call with the location, I'd go pick it up with some help and bury it in a snow bank until I can get the activity organized—usually within a couple of days.

3. Preparing the kids: You can't cut open a deer and start removing organs with all the blood and gore involved without desensitizing ten- and eleven-year-old kids. By assuring them that nothing I do to the deer can hurt them, showing them pictures of the various organs and explaining exactly what they will be experiencing generally takes care of it. I do, however, let them know that I won't force anyone to

watch. I do ask, however, that if they can't watch, they at least listen to what I'm saying during the process.

4. Where to do this: Obviously it wouldn't be a good idea to haul a dead deer into your classroom, plop it down on their desks, and start cutting it to pieces. I have been fortunate enough to be able to do this at the Trempealeau National Wildlife Refuge, either in a well-ventilated garage or outside, if the weather cooperates.

5. The actual dissection: The lesson plan included is pretty thorough and in the order I generally work. It isn't necessary to do everything I've included—any part of it is going to make it valuable, but more is better.

    –   I cut it wide open so they can see how everything goes together.

Me dissecting a two-and-a-half-year-old doe

– I show the lungs, and then cut into the trachea, pull the windpipe out, and actually blow into it so they can see the lungs expand. This is the grossest part of it, and you have to be careful. I got careless once, and it backed up on me. I nearly lost it, and I had to quickly turn away from the kids so they couldn't see my bloody, mucous-filled face (and also possibly see me throw up). I learned the hard way to have a needle nose pliers ready to pinch the trachea off before I quit blowing. The manager of the refuge was my assistant at the time and never quit teasing me about that one. Every year I did it after that, however, he was more than willing to help as long as "you're going to blow into the lungs."

  – I remove each of the major organs, cut into them, and talk about their function—heart, kidney, lung, liver.

  – I cut off a leg and pull on the tendon to show how it bends the leg.

  – I remove an eye and cut it open to show the lens.

  – I talk about the hair. It is actually hollow in the winter, which helps insulate the deer for warmth.

  – If it's a doe, there is likely a fetus (or two or three). Even a fawn of only six or eight months has a 40 percent chance of being impregnated and having a fetus. The first time they will have a single fawn but after that, they have either twins or even triplets.

  – The last thing I do is cut into the stomach. The smell tends to get pretty ripe after that so they won't want to stick around too long after.

Have a camera, as the process is educational, but the reactions of the kids (and even the adults) is worth capturing.

Photos by
Tom Hunter

Biology class outdoors

Trempealeau Elementary fifth graders got a real-life look at the inside of a deer to follow up on biology lessons on human organs. Teacher Scott Lee took the class to the Trempealeau National Wildlife Refuge Tuesday, December 16 to dissect a 1½ year old doe which had been killed by a car the night before. Lee says the deer is the only mammal with internal organs about the same size as those of the human. During the dissection, Lee discovered a 3 week old fetus.

Above right, Lee shows the students the doe's teeth. Looking on are, from the left, C.J. Pellowski, Wade Overson, and Travis Ritter. Bob Drieslein (back to the camera), refuge manager, helped Lee with the demonstration, offering additional knowledge and

One year, I was told by my principal that I couldn't do the dissection unless I did it with all three elementary schools in our district. I tried to explain that this just wouldn't work. It would involve me spending time with all the kids to desensitize them. I would have to do it three different times as that would be too many kids crammed in, and they wouldn't be able to see. I just couldn't do it justice with that many. Many years I couldn't get even one deer so the odds of getting three were pretty slim. I tried to explain that it certainly would be better for at least some of the kids to get the experience than not doing it at all. She and the other principal wouldn't back down so it looked like that activity was going to become a thing of the past.

I felt pretty strongly, however, and never have been one to back down on something I felt was right. A day or two later, I came across a dead deer on my way home, so thought it was meant to be. I called a teaching friend and had him meet me on the way to school the next day to load it in my pickup. We found a snow bank to bury it, and I went to school to get things organized. I set it up with the refuge to do it in the evening (the principal couldn't tell me I couldn't do it on my own time) and sent letters home with all the fifth graders, telling parents that this was happening, so bring your kids if it works out. I also got hold of a reporter friend for a local newspaper and let him know this was happening.

The night came and the turnout was incredible—nearly every fifth grader was there as well as dozens of parents. The reporter was also there, and two days later, he ran an article on the front page with three big colored photos and a nice article. The parents (including a mother who was the president of our PTO) realized what an incredibly educational activity this was and questioned the school as to why it had been stopped as a school activity. I didn't really gain any brownie points from my principal, of course, but it was all worth it.

News article after doing evening dissection

Deer Dissection

Scott Lee

Materials Needed
- sharp hunting-style knife—axe
- hacksaw rubber gloves
- drop cloth or plastic—bowl
- apron (or hospital gown)—camera
- needle nose pliers—bolt cutter
- roll of paper towel—funnel

Obtaining the Deer
- Make contact with local and county police to let them know that you're looking for a roadkill deer. No special permits are necessary, as they will tag it for you.
- Winter is the best time as the deer will not spoil as fast. In fact, a deer can be placed under a snow bank for an extended period of time (even a couple of weeks) and will neither spoil nor freeze too solidly to work with.

Preparing the Students
- They need to know, as much as possible, just exactly what they will be experiencing, as do their parents (it should be easy to justify to the parents as it is an outstanding lesson on organs of the body and how they function).
- Pictures or posters showing the insides of a deer (or another animal if you can't find a deer) should be shown (the DNR sometimes has these available for hunters to show how to field dress a deer).
- Give them the option of watching or staying in the back and only listening. Some may be quite queasy and need to step out on occasion to "get a breath of fresh air."

- Over 40,000 deer are killed by cars every year in the state of Wisconsin.
- Remind the students that no matter what you do to that deer, you are not hurting it—it will feel nothing. They must convince themselves of this and realize the problem will be in their heads. The deer is already dead!

Predissection Discussion (to discuss before opening deer)
- Wear gloves to avoid Lyme disease that can be spread through the blood. Deer ticks are in the egg stage in winter so it is not a concern but the blood is.
- Hair on deer is hollow as insulation, similar to thermopane windows. Their summer hair is different to keep them cooler.
- Talk about the "stress index" of deer. This can be determined by counting the number of days the weather gets below zero and the number of days the snow depth is over eighteen inches. If the total reaches eighty or more, there will be mass starvation of the deer population.
- A deer can lose up to 32 percent of its weight and still live but will die if it loses any more. The normal winter weight loss is about 20 percent. Deer have a seven-month gestation period. If the stress level gets too high, however, the fetus may be reabsorbed to avoid starvation.
- Point out similarities and differences of deer to us: similar size, mammal, etc. Differences include no gall bladder as it does not eat meat, it is a ruminant (cud chewer), and it is an ungulate (has split hoof).
- Has three sweat glands: (1) tarsal gland behind knee (which is actually the heel on a deer)—they urinate and it runs down the leg through the tarsal to the ground, leaving a distinct odor; (2) inter-digital between the hooves—leaves odor when scraping the ground; (3) preorbital on head between antlers—leaves odor when rubbing antlers on trees.
- Tail is raised as warning and lowered when in pain or to show submissiveness.

- Point out feet and legs. The entire lower leg is actually the foot—knee is really the heel. Show dew claws—back of leg just up from main hoof. (Both bucks and does have them.) Their toenails are carotene like our fingernails.
- Talk about their senses. They have excellent hearing as ears are large and can rotate. They can smell ten times better than us. The placement of their eyes enable them to see 270 degrees. They are not technically color blind but rather can see only one end of the spectrum—can see blues and greens but not orange, yellow, and red.

Dissecting the Deer
- Find a well-ventilated area such as a garage or even outside, weather permitting.
- Deer should be placed on its side on some type of "blood-proof" covering with students in a position where they can get a good look at the process.
- Look at jaw—can tell the age of the deer (see a chart for process of aging deer). Sawing across a tooth is the only exact way of aging but looking at jaw is fairly accurate.
- Be sure to wear rubber gloves, as deer are a primary carrier of Lyme disease and deer ticks that cause it.
- Remove skin along entire side from hip through neck.
- Cut off a piece of fat and explain that lots of fat means deer is in prime condition. (Talk about the "stress index" if you haven't already.)
- Cut off front leg and point out that there is no bone connecting it to the body. Saw the leg off below the "knee." If the marrow is white, it is healthy.
- Red means it is starving (pink—75 percent, yellow—50 percent). Take needle nose pliers, and grab tendon of leg to show how it controls bending of legs.
- Cut entire side open by using bolt cutter along backbone (cutting ribs), exposing as much of the inside of the deer as possible. (Be careful not to cut into any of the internal

organs.) Stuff paper towels into the body cavity to absorb as much blood as possible.

- Talk about function of the rib cage as protection and to assist in breathing. Take a rib, and break it to show how sharp they are—they can puncture the lung if broken.
- Show trachea (larger windpipe) and esophagus (smaller food passage). Cut them off in the neck. Push Phillip screwdriver through esophagus to show it's hollow and that it stretches. (Talk about food getting stuck but is usually released with drink of water. Heimlich is necessary when food is stuck in trachea, not esophagus.)
- Put small funnel into trachea (and be ready with needle nose pliers) and blow into it to show expansion of the lungs. Pinch off the trachea quickly when done blowing to avoid "backwash."
- Cut out the lungs and heart as one unit. Show the blue veins, which means blood doesn't have oxygen in it and red contains oxygen.
- Cut out the heart from between the lungs. Point out "heart" shape. Cut it open to show the four chambers as in our hearts. Two are atriums (top) that receive, and two are ventricles (bottom) that pump. Show blue veins on side of heart, and talk about bypass surgery—when veins are plugged by cholesterol, the surgeon will connect the veins around the plug.
- Show diaphragm ("skin" below the lungs and heart). It separates the respiratory from the digestive system. When you breathe in, the diaphragm goes down.
- Cut out the liver, which is the largest organ in the body (about three to four pounds). The function is to filter old, dead blood cells/bruises. It converts it to bile that breaks down fat. When cut open, it looks like a filter.
- Cut out the kidneys, which are covered with fat if deer is healthy. There are two, but if one fails, the other will grow larger. They filter waste to bladder (urine). You can live only three days without kidneys unless you have a trans-

plant or go on dialysis. When cut open, they look like a filter. (They are shaped like a kidney bean.)

- Cut off back leg to show ball and socket joint. There is bone to cut through to remove back leg.
- Show stomach (don't cut into it yet). Food enters it via the esophagus. Digestive fluids are added to change solids into a thick, soupy substance.
- Show small intestines—ours are about fifteen to twenty feet long. They must be all wound up, or we would have to be over twenty feet tall. (Some animals such as snakes, worms, and eel are stretched out their length.) Their function is to pull energy from food into the blood.
- Show large intestines—about four to six feet long. They pull the water out of the waste entering from the small intestines. If they don't function correctly, we would have constant diarrhea and would become dehydrated.
- If a doe, look for a fetus—nearly every adult doe will be pregnant (conception takes place in November and December and birth is in May and June). Even about 40 percent of the yearlings (fawns) will be carrying young. The first birth will be single, but the rest will nearly always be twins or even triplets.
- Cut out an eye—dissect it, show the different parts, and put it into a bowl to pass around. Eyes have rods or cones but cannot have 100 percent of both. If an animal has mainly rods, they don't see color but have excellent night vision as in deer. If mainly cones, they see color and have good day vision as in people. Deer have mostly rods but some cones—can see blues and greens but not oranges or reds. Show lens, which looks like contacts—flips image upside down and the brain turns it back again.
- Cut into brain and take out one side by scraping it away from the cavity—show the small size and what it looks like. There are not nerve cells; therefore, it feels no pain. Right side of the brain controls the left side of the body and vice

versa. (It is actually the third crash that kills: [1] car hits tree, [2] head hits object, and [3] brain hits inside of skull.)

– Cut into the stomach—try to determine what the deer has been eating: corn, stems, buds, etc. A deer has four chambers to its stomachs, similar to a cow (there will be more of a smell, so save this until last).

Disposal of the Deer

The carcass can either be given to someone who wants the meat (they should also have their name on the tag from the DNR or police), or it can be put out into the woods. Many animals (fox, coyote, woodpeckers, chickadees, other birds, etc.) will welcome the easy meal through the difficult winters.

Chapter 19
Keep on Singin'

Several of us on the staff, especially Cheri, Selis, and I, were in to changing the words of various songs to fit whatever might be going on in school—baby and wedding showers, can collection results, staff get-togethers, retirement parties, whatever reason to come up with a song. I especially got into it around the holidays for our annual Christmas party. For many years, I would come up with songs and create a sing-along songbook with various staff members as "victims." Songs such as "Clifford, the Red-Nosed Principal," "No Christmas Tree" (our administration decided one year to ban them in our classroom), "I'm Dreaming of a New School Board," "Computer Hell" (early intros to computers to a group of us technological zeroes), "Oh Table A" (to the tune "Oh Christmas Tree"), "Whisper Wonderland," "Jolly Old Saint (insert current superintendent), "Please," and more.

My personal favorite was "Dingy Gals" to the tune of Jingle Bells. The words are below and will give you an idea of the flavor of the various songs. With this one, it would start out with a nice, mixed choir, but as the song progresses, the soprano and alto sections slowly disappears, while the tenor and bass sections get louder. By the end, as you might imagine, it was an all-men's chorus of male staff and husbands singing quite merrily. Yeah, maybe rather sexist, but I prefer to call it a little revenge for what I often had to put up with at Table A.

Dashing through the school,
It's obvious to all,
There are dingy women,
Wandering through the hall.
Sandys, Debs, Jo, Di,
Pam, Val, and Carolyn,
Selis, Janes, Donna, Cheri, Darlene,
Betsy, Margaret, Marilyn,
—OOOOOOOOOOOOOH—
Dingy Gals, Dingy Gals,
Our staff has a bunch!
Everybody must agree,
They're really out to lunch.
Dingy Gals, Dingy Gals,
Our staff has a lot!
Luckily they're also blessed
With Tom, Dave, John, and Scott!

Part Three

• •

Refuge Fun Facts and Activities

I have been a member of the Board of Directors for the Friends of the Trempealeau National Wildlife Refuge since it was created, always serving as either President or Vice President. The refuge has been my favorite natural place in the whole world, and I spend as much time out there as I possibly can. I know the place extremely well.

For the past seven years, we have published a quarterly newsletter that comes out at the beginning of each season. I was asked to write an article for each addition and chose to write it on "Fun Facts about Our Local Wildlife." I've chosen a variety of topics ranging from migration to hibernation, frogs to birds, leaf pounding to snow ice cream, and quizzes to "hink pinks." The following pages are those I've written to date. They may deal directly to the Trempealeau National Wildlife Refuge, but the facts are accurate for that specific critter/subject no matter where it is found.

Chapter 20
"The Tongue of All Tongues"

(Summer)

A woodpecker's tongue is about four times the length of its beak and barbed at the end. When it flicks its tongue out, it can, therefore, stab and hold onto the insect/larva as it pulls it in. The problem, however, is where does all that tongue go without choking him/her? The solution: it is actually attached on the top of its skull and is somewhat elastic so the tongue is pulled back through its mouth, splits to go around the spine, and goes up under the feathers/skin to be stored on top of its skull. Problem solved!

"Woodpecker tree"
(Part of thirty-foot display case at Trempealeau Elementary School)

Birds *do not* migrate to avoid the cold? They are well-adapted to tolerate the extreme upper Midwestern winters. Unfortunately, their food is not always so tolerant. For the birds reliant on those food sources, they must migrate to where they can find food. For example, insect eaters must find a warm enough climate for insects to survive (an exception being those woodpeckers that are adapted to get at hibernating insects), or fish-eating birds must go to where the water doesn't freeze so they can get at those fish (or adapt to another food type such as bald eagles switching over to carrion instead of fish).

Chapter 21
"What a Trip!"

(Autumn)

The tundra swans that migrate through the refuge from mid-October through November each year are on their way from their nesting grounds in the Arctic tundra region of Canada and Alaska. They are heading to their wintering grounds on the east coasts of Delaware, Virginia, and North Carolina, with a huge concentration on Chesapeake Bay. This is a journey of about four thousand miles! The refuge is a great place to view the swans, as well as right along the highway just south of Brownsville, Minnesota.

By the way, have you noticed that when swans and other waterfowl fly in their "V" formation that one line of the "V" is almost always longer than the other? Do you know the reason?*

Tundra swans
(Photo taken at Trempealeau Lakes)

*(It's because there are more birds in one line! ☺)

Chapter 22
"Whooo Said That?"

(Winter)

Soon you may start hearing an increase of owls calling. They are very territorial and will use their hooting or other calls to establish these territories for nesting and protecting their hunting areas. As the most common owls found in the refuge, great horned and barred, will be on their nest by late winter (as early as late January for the great horned and not too long after for the barred, with eggs hatching in early and late March respectively), they want these territorial boundaries well-defined before then. Although we often hear of hoot owls, there really is no such critter. There are owls that hoot, such as the great horned and barred (and also those that "just don't give a hoot," I guess ☺), but not "hoot owls."

Saw whet owl with deer mouse in its talons
(Photo taken near Winona, Minnesota)

They're not the easiest critter to see, but listening for these hoots might help. Especially after the leaves fall in the autumn and throughout the winter and early spring, they need to find places to hide out during the daytime. The best spots are in groves of evergreen trees. When you hear hooting, look for some evergreen trees in that area, and that will be your best bet for finding one. It's tougher finding them once the deciduous trees leaf out, as they are able to spread around. They do tend to stick to their established territories, however, so they will still spend a lot of their time in those evergreens, and even the same tree. I once found seventy-nine owl pellets under one tree, and watching me from above was a great horned owl. I revisited that tree often, and there were always owl pellets underneath, and I got to see the source numerous times.

News article on Tom and I doing some "owling"

Chapter 23
"Gold or Not So Gold"

(Spring)

You will soon be noticing that the bright yellow and black American goldfinch showing up around the refuge and at your feeders, but guess what—they probably never left! The male goldfinch only has those bright colors during their mating season, spring and through the summer. Once the mating/nesting is over, they have no need for those bright colors to attract a mate. In fact, it can be very dangerous for them, as they are much more visible to predators. Come fall and through the winter, you will see them with a much more bland, camouflaged color and are difficult to distinguish from the females. Being seedeaters, they do not need to migrate to find food, so will be here year-round.

American goldfinch
(Male in summer, female, male in winter)
(Part of thirty-foot display case at Trempealeau Elementary)

Chapter 24
Not Just a "Bunch"

How about a little quiz to test your knowledge on some of the critters you might find at the refuge? Can you match up the following critter in the left column with what you would call a group of those critters in the right column? The answers can be found on the next page.*

Badger	charm
Bat	gaggle
Beaver	swarm
Butterfly	cloud
Coyote	pod
Crane	scurry
Crow	rafter
Deer	surfeit
Dragonfly	kettle
Duck	pack
Eagle	cloud
Fox	sedge
Frog	herd
Goldfinch	chattering
Goose	prickle
Grasshopper	lamentation
Grouse	flock
Hawk (migrating)	cete
Mosquito	murder
Owl	leash
Pelican	covey
Porcupine	flutter
Skunk	army
Squirrel	convocation
Starling	family
Swan	cluster
Turkey	parliament

Canada geese and goslings—a "gaggle of geese"
(Photo taken at Trempealeau National Wildlife Refuge [TNWR])

*Answers to matching quiz:

badger/cete, bat/cloud, beaver/family, butterfly/flutter, coyote/pack, crane/sedge, crow/murder, deer/herd, dragonfly/cluster, duck/flock, eagle/convocation, fox/leash, frog/army, goldfinch/charm, goose/gaggle, grasshopper/cloud, grouse/covey, hawk (migrating)/kettle, mosquito/swarm, owl/parliament, pelican/pod, porcupine/prickle, skunk/surfeit, squirrel/scurry, starling/chattering, swan/lamentation, turkey/rafter

Chapter 25
"Baby" Just Won't Cut It!

Another quiz to test your knowledge—this time matching some of the critters you might find at the refuge with what their young are called. Can you match up the following critter with what you would call their babies (such as a cow's baby is a calf)? Some might have the same name or more than one correct name. The answers can be found on the next page.*

_____ Badger	A. nymph
_____ Bat	B. tadpole
_____ Beaver	C. spiderling
_____ Cormorant	D. kit
_____ Coyote	E. joey
_____ Crane	F. duckling
_____ Deer	G. kit
_____ Dragonfly	H. whelp
_____ Eagle	I. fawn
_____ Fox	J. neonate
_____ Frog	K. wriggler
_____ Goose	L. toadlet
_____ Hawk	M. pup
_____ Mallard	N. kit
_____ Mosquito	O. hatchling
_____ Opossum	P. eaglet
_____ Otter	Q. pup
_____ Owl	R. squab
_____ Pigeon	S. eyas
_____ Rabbit	T. shaglet
_____ Skunk	U. poult
_____ Snake	V. owlet
_____ Spider	W. gosling
_____ Toad	X. cub
_____ Turkey	Y. colt
_____ Turtle	Z. bunny

Whitetail deer fawn
(Photo taken at TNWR)

*Answers to matching quiz:

badger/kit (or cub), bat/pup, beaver/kit (or pup), cormorant/shaglet, coyote/pup (or cub or whelp), crane/colt, deer/fawn, dragonfly/nymph, eagle/eaglet, fox/kit (or cub or pup), frog/tadpole, goose/gosling, hawk/eyas, mallard/duckling, mosquito/wriggler (or nymph), opossum/joey, otter/whelp (or pup), owl/owlet, pigeon/squab, rabbit/bunny, skunk/kit, snake/neonate, spider/spiderling, toad/toadlet (or tadpole), turkey/poult, turtle/hatchling

Chapter 26
"Eating Poison?"

(Summer)

Through all four stages of the *Monarch butterfly's life,* they are dependent on milkweed for their survival. The butterfly will lay its *eggs* on the underside of a milkweed leaf. About four days later, it hatches into the *larva/caterpillar* stage, where it has a convenient source of food with this milkweed plant. After about two weeks, the caterpillar will then attach itself to the milkweed, or nearby plant, to form the *chrysalis/pupa.* About ten days later, when the *butterfly* emerges, it will move on to other food sources (nectar from a variety of flowers) but even in this final stage, it would be in great peril had it not been for the milkweed. The "milk" from milkweed is toxic! Monarchs, however, are immune from this poison and having it in their system gives them a horrible taste, protecting them from potential predators.

These beautiful Monarch butterflies are in trouble, however, and need us desperately to help them out! The reason stems primarily from the loss of milkweed, which is caused by such things as farms taking more and more milkweed habitat for crops plus the overuse of chemicals to kill "weeds." These chemicals are used on farm fields, where the wind may be a factor in affecting milkweed, and also along roadsides, a common habitat for the milkweed. We all can help by not only discouraging this often unnecessary and careless use of chemicals and habitat destruction, but also by planting milkweed around our homes. Both Common Milkweed and Marsh Milkweed seem to be the easiest to grow in our area.

Monarch butterfly on blazing star
(Photo taken at TNWR)

Chapter 27
"The Migration Interpretation"

(Autumn)

When the fall migration is in full swing, some questions might come to mind as to the "why" and "how" this happens.

As to the "why," it is not because of the cold, as mentioned earlier, but rather because of a lack of food. Critters can generally adapt to and tolerate the cold weather, but can't last without a source of food. Therefore, if their food disappears (for reasons such as insects and smaller mammals hibernating or lakes and rivers freezing over), those animals that depend on them must move to a place where they can still be found.

The "how" is still a great mystery of science, although scientists are getting much closer to understanding this mystery. One idea to explain it is using the *sun as a compass.* Since the sun changes position as the Earth rotates, however, these critters must make adjustments. This method of migration is used mainly by animals that migrate during the day. The *stars* can also be used as a compass for those migrating primarily at night, taking advantage of various constellations (Big and Little Dipper, Draco the Dragon, Cassiopeia, etc.) that rotate around the North Star (Polaris). *Polarized light* from special light waves creating a pattern in the sky that stays the same as the sun moves across the sky is another method being studied and seems to be used not only by birds but also insects, amphibians, and fish. *Landscape maps,* of course, is also a great method for animals to get where they want to go, much like we use landscape clues to navigate around our neighborhoods.

All mysteries of how migrating animals find their way are not completely understood. How many of us could find our way hundreds or even thousands of miles without our GPS or maps? How can we not love and respect these marvelous critters?

Chapter 28
"To Hibernate or Not to Hibernate, That Is the Question"

(Winter)

As in migration, hibernation is not determined by the cold nearly as much as it is by food supply. With their thick fur, mammals can do a pretty good job of tolerating the cold of our winters, but no critter can tolerate a lack of food. Even the big black bear with its heavy fur can't survive without its diet of mostly plants (nuts, berries, etc.) and insects. What little meat it does rely on for food isn't enough for them to survive the long winters. The option: hibernation. A pretty remarkable adaptation!

How about the beaver (and also the muskrat)? The water freezes and they, being mammals, can't breathe under water so their choice must be hibernation, right? Wrong—they remain active all winter underneath that frozen pond. So how can they manage that? For one thing, they must "plan ahead." They can't hold their breath all winter, so must have a way to get above the water level. That happens by building a home where they can get to air, as they'd likely have migraines all winter trying to break through the ice for air. Their cone-shaped homes of sticks, grasses, and mud are built in shallow water but not so shallow that the water will freeze to the bottom (their remarkable dam-building helps guarantee the correct water depth). Their main living space is above the water (ice) but, as they feed under the water, there has to be tunnels going below the ice.

As they are herbivores (plant eaters), how do they find those yummy plants in the winter? Again, they must "plan ahead." By chewing on the trees and shrubs near the water and engineering them to fall into the water (and "engineers" they are), the leaves and inner bark help supplement their diets throughout the winter. Being able to hold their breath a whole lot longer than us also makes all this food-gathering much more doable.

The beaver has many more incredible adaptations,
but that's for another chapter.
Beaver
(Photo by Allen Blake Sheldon, Trempealeau)

Chapter 29
"There's More to Ducks than What Meets the Eye"

(Spring)

Waterfowl migration is in full swing as the ice is out and the nice, fresh backwaters are "open for business." As the spring advances, it'll be hard to look anywhere on the waters of the refuge without seeing ducks, as well as geese, swans, pelicans, and other waterfowl.

These *ducks have incredible adaptations* to help them get through life:

- Their *feet* are webbed not only to assist in swimming but also to keep them from sinking into the mud. They can spread them out for balance on land, and they also have "toenails" for gripping while on logs or even in trees like the wood duck.
- They are *well-camouflaged* (especially the females for protection on the nests). They are generally darker on the top, which makes it more difficult to be seen by predators from above, and lighter on the bottom, which is harder to be seen by a predator from below (such as fish and snapping turtles), as they look up toward the surface and sky.
- Their *bills* are spoon-shaped for scooping up food such as duckweed. They are also able to filter water out the sides without letting that duckweed "escape," avoiding a stomach full of water with little food.

– Their outer *feathers* have an oil on them to repel water and their inner, down feathers keep them warm. They don't need to migrate south for warmth, as these down feathers take care of that, but rather migrate to find sources of food when they can no longer find open water.

Wood duck
(From eighteen-foot waterfowl case at Trempealeau Elementary)

Chapter 30
"Adapted to Thrive"

(Summer)

Ah, those *squirrels!* They seem to be both loved and hated by many of us. If you feed the birds during the winters, hate may be your chosen adjective. Sometimes it feels like the majority of the birdseed that we spend all that money on gets eaten by the squirrels, rather than the birds it's intended for. But how can you not love their cuteness, persistence, and cleverness in their pursuit of that food source? "Squirrel-proof" feeders? Don't believe a word of it!

This is another critter that has some remarkable adaptations. They have very sharp front *teeth*/incisors with extremely strong *jaws*, enabling them to open up all those nuts to get at the nutmeat. If you don't believe that, just try biting into a walnut sometime. Actually, that may not be such a great idea as the only one that'll be happy with that will be your dentist! The rusty brown color is not from poor dental hygiene, but rather makes their teeth much tougher and longer-lasting, as well as good camouflage, as their mouths are opened a lot. Their teeth, like all rodents, grow constantly as they would otherwise wear down with all the hard objects they eat.

Me with young gray squirrel
(Photo taken on camping trip with students
at Perrot State Park, Trempealeau)

Their *tails* have a variety of uses: it provides balance while on small limbs and highline wires, as well as when sitting on their hind legs, it fluffs up to serve as a "parachute" while jumping from tree to tree. It's used as a "warning" to other squirrels by wiggling it, and it even serves as an "umbrella" when they put it over their heads during rainy days.

Their smaller *front feet* are used to hold their food and also for digging to bury nuts to help them get through the long winters. They can actually *smell* these buried nuts through a foot of snow! The larger *back feet* are great for jumping, balancing, and holding on to the trees.

I'm not saying you have to love them, but how can we not at least respect and appreciate all these remarkable survival skills they possess?

Chapter 31
"Pounding Leaves?"

(Autumn)

Ah, autumn along the Mississippi River! How can you not love it? The migration down the Mississippi Flyway in full swing, critters preparing to get through the winter, mosquito-free hiking, cooler (and not yet cold) temperatures, and, of course, the beautiful fall colors, definitely *my* favorite season, and I'm guessing, many of yours. It's definitely *not* the season to stay inside. Get out there and enjoy it.

How about a fun little activity that can be enjoyed by all ages: "Leaf Pounding" (creating leaf prints).

Things you need:
- cotton fabric about eight-inch square (cutting up an old white sheet works great or you can purchase material at any fabric store)
- hammer, table salt, and water
- small tub / medium-size bowl, white paper (computer paper)
- newspaper and, of course, some pretty leaves

Directions:
- Collect some leaves—green or those turning color (not dead).
- Place a leaf, underside down, onto the piece of fabric.
- Fold the white paper around the leaf and fabric.
- Fold newspaper around it all.
- Place on a hard, flat surface and start pounding, making sure you're hitting all parts of where the leaf is hidden under the paper.
- When done, dip the leaf-printed fabric into the tub/bowl of saltwater solution to set the colors.

It's a fun, artsy little activity the entire family can enjoy, and it can all be done outside. Enjoy and have a wonderful autumn, and put the arrival of winter-soon-to-come out of your minds. It makes the fall even easier to appreciate.

First Peak, a.k.a. Liberty Peak, Trempealeau
(Photo taken near river below bluff)

Chapter 32
Frozen Solid and Still Alive?

(Winter)

Frogs, like all critters, must have special adaptations to survive in a varied climate like we have here. The wood frog, named because it likes to "hang out" in small woodland ponds common to the refuge, have to find a way to survive until spring. Hibernating in these shallow ponds—that will likely freeze solid into the ground below—should be a death sentence. As they freeze, however, they draw in their legs and tuck their digits under their body. This position helps keep them from drying out over the winter. They will actually freeze solid, turning into little "frogsicles" with no heartbeat or brain activity. Then come spring and presto—they thaw out and continue their life cycle, sometimes actually calling (a quacking sound) for a mate while there's snow still on the ground. Maybe the "Rip Van Winkle frog" might be a better name? Scientists interested in cryogenics study these amazing little critters in hopes of learning how they can perfect this process in humans.

When you hear frogs "croaking," it is only the males you're hearing. What a life—the males just sit back and make their special sounds, and the females come hopping or swimming up for their evening of romance. Maybe in my next life, I'll try to come back as a frog!

Mating Eastern Gray Tree Frogs
(Photo taken near Trempealeau)

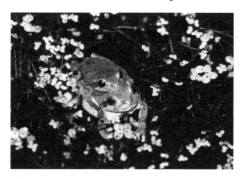

Frogs don't "croak," however. For example, spring peepers "peep," wood frogs "quack," tree frogs "chirp," leopard frogs "snore," American toads have a sort of "whistling hum," bull frogs sound like a viola, but none of our frogs or toads make a croaking sound. They also make their vocalizations during different times of the spring and summer. Their timing is based on water temperature. The wood frogs are the earliest and can even, as mentioned, be out "quacking" when there's still snow on the ground. Spring peepers, chorus frogs, leopard frogs, toads, and tree frogs follow along as the spring and early summer arrive. Last, but not least, come the green and (rarely heard around here) bull frogs, which need the warmest waters for mating.

Eastern gray tree frog and American toad doing his whistling hum
(Photo taken near Trempealeau)

Chapter 33
"What's with the Knobby Nose?"

(Spring)

The American white pelican are common visitors to the refuge and are already showing up by midspring. When you see them, pay attention to their beaks. If they have a big, orange knob on their beak, it means they are breeding birds, so will not stay around too long. Most of them will head further north to breed and nest—northern Wisconsin and Minnesota or into Canada. You might notice that many pelicans will stick around all summer, however. These are birds that are either too young or too old to breed so stay here at the refuge, taking advantage of the prime habitat available to them. They will move up and down the river in this area during the days to feed on fish in various backwaters, but many spend at least the nights in the refuge wetlands.

Watching a flock of them in flight is a wonder to behold. It reminds me of a ballet in the sky, as they soar gracefully above in synchronized circles to catch the thermals. Even flying low along the water, it is amazing how infrequently they have to flap their wings. Their huge wings are an incredible adaptation for saving energy in flight.

White pelican
(Photo by Allen Blake Sheldon, Trempealeau)

Chapter 34
"Can You Do Better than Boy and Girl?"

Another quiz to test your knowledge—this time matching some of the critters you might find at the refuge (or could have in the past) with what the male and female of that species are called. Can you match up the following critters with what you would call the male and female (such as goats would be called Billy and Nanny)? The answers can be found on the next page.*

_____ Badger	A. Drake and Hen
_____ Bee	B. Jack and Jill
_____ Coyote	C. Buck and Doe
_____ Dragonfly	D. Gander and Goose
_____ Duck	E. Tom and Jenny
_____ Elk	F. Drone and Queen
_____ Fox	G. Tiercel and Hen
_____ Goose	H. Boar and Sow
_____ Hawk	I. Bull and Cow
_____ Opossum	J. Dog and Bitch
_____ Pheasant	K. King and Queen
_____ Turkey	L. Tod and Vixen
_____ Whitetail Deer	M. Cock and Hen

Red Fox "Vixen"
(Photo taken in my backyard in Trempealeau)

*Answers to matching quiz:

H. Badger (Boar and Sow) / L. Fox (Tod and Vixen) / F. Bee (Drone and Queen) / D. Goose (Gander and Goose) / J. Coyote (Dog and Bitch) / G. Hawk (Tiercel and Hen) / K. Dragonfly (King and Queen) / B. Opossum (Jack and Jill) / A. Duck (Drake and Hen) / M. Pheasant (Cock and Hen) / I. Elk (Bull and Cow) / E. Turkey (Tom and Jenny) / C. Whitetail Deer (Buck and Doe)

Chapter 35
"Hink Pinks"

How are you at "hink pinks?" So just what is a hink pink? They're two rhyming words that fit for the definition given. For example, a large hog (1) would be a "big pig" or my bathroom (2) would be "Scotty's potty" or my happiness (3) would be "Lee's glee." (The number after the clue tells you how many syllables in each word.) Okay, try these, all of which refer to critters you might find in the refuge. The answers can be found on the next page.*

1. a phobia of bucks and does (1)
2. a morning full of baby deer (1)
3. a light red weasel (1)
4. the spinning of a certain tree rodent (2)
5. a very pregnant-prone shelled reptile (2)
6. a female, big-mouthed fish (1)
7. a sandhill's "owie" (1)
8. a honker in need of some tightening (1)
9. an orange-breasted bird's sewing accessary (2)
10. a shivering rattler (2)
11. an entire ground rodent (1)
12. a waterfowl's chicken imitation (1)
13. a fowl with some odd behaviors (2)
14. get hold of it, Mr. Hare (2)
15. the masked mammal will be here in a bit (2)
16. an amphibian's daily computer entry (1)
17. an ailing Lyme carrier (1)
18. a chubby flying mammal (1)
19. a very unselfish cousin to the egret (2)
20. an amphibian's highway (1)
21. say it once more, big white waterfowl (3)
22. the woodchuck's tied up pet canine (2)
23. a pretend male mallard (1)

Mating northern water snakes (shakey snakeys)
(Photo taken at TNWR)

*Answers to "Hink Pinks:"

(1) deer fear, (2) fawn dawn, (3) pink mink, (4) squirrel's twirl, (5) fertile turtle, (6) bass lass, (7) crane's pain, (8) loose goose, (9) robin's bobbin, (10) shakey snakey, (11) whole mole, (12) duck cluck, (13) quirkey turkey, (14) grab it rabbit, (15) raccoon's back soon, (16) frog's blog, (17) sick tick, (18) fat bat, (19) sharin' heron, (20) toad's road, (21) tell again, pelican, (22) ground hog's bound dog, (23) fake drake

Chapter 36
"Snow Ice Cream"

(Winter)

Yes, winter will come—and soon! You do live in the Midwest, you know. How about some ice cream to help survive the winter? Better yet, how about some "snow ice cream!" Here's a "kid-tested" recipe you might want to try:

- Mix 2 eggs, 1 cup of sugar, and 1/2 teaspoon of salt together until it's creamy.
- In separate bowl mix 2/3 cup of milk, and 1 tablespoon of vanilla together.
- Combine the two mixtures and beat them together.
- Pour this mixture over 12 cups of snow (the fresh, fluffy, clean, *white* stuff!). Fold it in quickly before the snow melts. Add more snow to make it thicker or if it is too sweet.

    (It's best to eat it outside, as it gets watery quickly in warm temperatures)

Another option, but not quite as fun, as it doesn't involve snow, is some "Ice Cream in a Bag":

- Mix 8 ounces / 1 cup of milk, 1 teaspoon of vanilla, and 2 teaspoons of sugar together in a ziplock sandwich bag.
- Fill a one-gallon ziplock bag with ice and dump in a generous portion of salt.
- Zip the small bag shut tightly, and put it into the large bag of ice/salt mixture.

    –   Shake them until the mixture in the small bag hardens to desired texture. (You'll want gloves for this part.)

(2 percent or whole milk works best and chocolate milk is an option.)

Get out the spoon and dip into that small bag (but keep in mind that outside the bag will be salty).

Chapter 37
"Why Poison Them When You Can Eat Them?"

(Spring)

So just what comes to mind when you think of "dandelions," weeds, pests? Disgusting? Kill them at all costs? Lawn ruiners? Well, it's time to take a closer look and maybe do some rethinking in our dealings with those "miserable" dandelions!

Dandelions (from a French word pronounced [dent' day lay own], meaning "tooth of the lion" because of their tooth-shaped leaves) are actually very edible and, in fact, are better for you, containing more vitamins and nutrients than the majority of vegetables you might buy at the grocery store. Not only that, but you can eat all parts of them except the stems. The flowers, buds, and leaves can be eaten as a salad while you can grind up the roots to make a coffee-like drink. Dandelion fritters are really good, simply dipping the flowers and buds in a pancake/beer batter and deep fat frying them like you might do with fish or onion rings.

Dandelion

You maybe should know, however, that the words "edible" and "yummy" are not synonyms. "Edible" means you can eat it without negative impacts; "yummy," of course, means the same—but they also taste good! If dandelions could only add that "yummy" aspect, they'd likely be a best seller, and you'd be harvesting them from your yards instead of spraying to kill them off. A precaution: always wash them good first and don't eat dandelions or anything if there is any chance they've been sprayed with a pesticide or weed killer!

Here are some tips that might help with that "yummy" part. The key to a good salad, in my opinion, is *lots* of a favorite salad dressing, so keep that in mind! Dipping those fritters in a little powdered sugar before eating them helps, although they're pretty good even without the powdered sugar! As far as the coffee-like ground up roots, I've never found a way to make *anything* "coffee-like" taste good, despite my Norwegian heritage—sorry! If you're like me, you may have better luck by adding a little milk and lots of sugar—but I still won't drink it. Enjoy your new spring diet!

Chapter 38
"What the Heck Is an Ebony Avian?"

How about a little ornithology quiz on bird names? Can you figure out the name of the following birds found at the refuge? (For example, "a coward from the great plains" would be a prairie chicken.) The answers can be found on the next page.*

What common refuge bird name has the same name as the following:

1.   a baseball outfielder? _____
2.   what thieves are doin'? _____
3.   a regal angler? _____
4.   a sad letter? _____
5.   a sad peace-lover? _____
6.   seeing with a precious metal? _____
7.   preceding digestion? _____
8.   an avian milk giver? _____
9.   murdering a game animal? _____
10. the pope's "assistant"? _____
11. construction equipment used on dunes? _____
12. an extra line of chairs at a concert? _____
13. an ebony avian? _____
14. the rear of a painter's cloth? _____
15. a Maryland baseball player? _____

Baby American Robin
(Photo taken near Trempealeau Hotel)

*Answers to ornithology name quiz:

(1) flycatcher, (2) robin, (3) kingfisher, (4) blue jay, (5) mourning dove, (6) goldeneye, (7) swallow, (8) cowbird, (9) killdeer, (10) cardinal, (11) sandhill crane, (12) song sparrow, (13) blackbird, (14) canvasback, (15) Baltimore oriole

Chapter 39
"The Butcher Bird"

(Winter)

You may notice a "new" bird hanging around this winter. When we think of migration, we tend to think of the birds heading south where it's nice and warm. That's not always the case as some birds, such as the *northern shrike* (a light gray and white bird with a black mask and a little smaller than a robin) seem to think this area is nice and warm, as this is where many end up in the winter, coming down from further north.

Northern shrike
(From thirty-foot display case at Trempealeau Elementary School)

The northern shrike's main diet is smaller birds. Many of these birds head south for the winter. The shrikes tend to do the same thing, leaving us as the "south" they need. They're most likely to be found near marshy areas and like to perch high up on trees to get a better view of potential food.

The nickname you might hear for them is the "butcher bird." This comes from their unique way of catching their prey. If you look close, you will see they have a raptor-like, hooked beak. This tells you that they eat other animals, as the beak is used for tearing the prey apart before eating. Unlike raptors that eat live animals, however, they don't have the strong, sharp talons, which are used for killing their prey before eating. Turkey vultures are the only raptors found around here that do not have those talons as they eat dead animals, so they don't have to kill their prey before eating it. Shrikes are not raptors, but they do eat live birds. They must, therefore, find another way to kill their prey as their wimpy feet aren't good for much except perching on a branch. What they do is catch the bird in their beaks, which are not big and strong enough to kill it, and quickly find a tree or bush with thorns (or a barb-wired fence) and impale the bird. They then use those perch-appropriate feet to get comfortable while using their raptor-like beak to tear it into swallow-size bites. The butcher bird nickname seems to fit.

Chapter 40
"Critter Hink Pinks"

How about some more "hink pinks?" In case you forgot what a "hink pink" is, they're two rhyming words that fit for the definition given. For example, a feline's gloves (2) would be a "kitten's mittens" or me in 90 degree weather (1) would be "hot Scott" or my urination (1) would be "Lee's pee." (The number after the clue tells you how many syllables in each word.) Okay, try these, all of which refer to critters you might find in the refuge. The answers can be found on the next page.*

Mammals
1. two large omnivores (1)
2. home of a small rodent (1)
3. a large weasel that works with clay (2)
4. a young, female tree-dwelling rodent (2)
5. the mild addiction of a larger rodent (2)
6. the odor of a medium-size weasel (1)
7. fuel used to heat an underground rodent's home (1)

Reptiles/Amphibians
8. a snake that always tells on his friends (2)
9. a snake that gives his life for a cause (2)
10. a snake's investment certificates (1)
11. an amphibian's favorite Christmas drink (1)
12. a highway for a warty critter (1)
13. a freshly showered larger frog (1)

Insects/Bugs
14. an eight-legged, bloodsucker's favorite ink pen (1)
15. one who leads arachnids around unfamiliar territory (2)

16. the urine of a dog lover's insect (1)
17. a dishonest blood-sucking insect (2)
18. the droppings of a tiny, annoying insect (1)

Birds
19. the "butcher bird's" complaint (1)
20. waterfowl good fortune (1)
21. a nonnative blackbird's girlfriend (2)
22. an accipiter's trance (2)
23. baby bird's choice (1)
24. thin white-throated or chipping (2)

Red "girl squirrel"
(Photo taken from my deck in Trempealeau)

*Answers to "Critter Hink Pinks":

(1) bear pair (and yes, there was a bear spotted in the refuge a few years ago), (2) mouse house, (3) otter potter, (4) girl squirrel, (5) rabbit's habit, (6) mink's stink, (7) mole coal, (8) rattler tattler, (9) garter martyr, (10) fox stocks, (11) frog nog, (12) toad road, (13) clean green, (14) tick's Bic, (15) spider guider, (16) flea's pee, (17) cheater skeeter, (18) gnat scat, (19) snipe's gripe, (20) duck luck, (21) starling's darling, (22) cooper's stupor, (23) chick's pick, (24) narrow sparrow

Chapter 41
"Is That the Same Deer?"

(Summer)

Have you noticed how much "skinnier" deer seem to be in the summer? Like us, they need to cut down on the "clothing" they wear as the temperatures rise (a deer's version of the bikini) and change to heavier clothing as it gets colder (their long johns). They do this by adapting the hair on their bodies for the season. Come fall, you'll see them appear to be putting on weight, but much of that "weight gain" is really just the change in their fur. A deer's winter fur is actually hollow, therefore, bigger. This provides an insulation that traps the heat, similar to us dressing in layers of clothing to trap the heat in between the layers or using thermal pane windows in our houses. During a snowstorm they will bed down and are often nearly covered with snow. When they get up, however, you would see that their fur is not wet like you'd expect as this insulated fur keeps their body heat from escaping and melting the snow—certainly a huge asset for a critter that can't come indoors and sit by the fireplace to wait out the storm.

In the summer, however, it's important that their fur does not cause them to overheat. They, therefore, shed this hollow, warmer fur and grow lighter weight fur that will keep them cooler during the hot summer days. You may also notice a difference in color from winter to summer. That summer fur has almost a reddish tint to it, while in the winter it's much browner.

This is just one of the many adaptations our wonderful whitetails have to survive—more to come in the next pages.

Whitetail buck in velvet
(Photo in their summer fur by Allen Blake Sheldon, Trempealeau)

Chapter 42
"Antlers and Rubs and Scrapes—Oh My"

(Autumn)

Our whitetail deer, so common at the refuge, have other interesting adaptations besides the fur mentioned in the last chapter. The fall is a great time to take notice of a couple of them.

You've likely noticed that the bucks are now growing back their *antlers* that they shed late last winter. There is a difference between "antlers" and "horns." Antlers are shed annually and grown back later in the year (such as deer, elk, and moose), while horns are permanent (such as bighorn sheep and goats). When they grow back, the texture is velvety. This velvet is actually blood vessels that will dry up when the antlers are fully grown.

Whitetail bucks in velvet
(Photo by Carne Lee at TNWR)

The deer then rub their antlers against small trees to scrape off the velvet and shine up their antlers to impress the ladies. They have a scent gland near the base of their antlers so while rubbing them against the tree, they are leaving a distinctive odor to let other bucks know that this is their territory. They also leave a visible mark by scraping the bark off the tree. Watch for these *buck rubs* as you're hiking.

You may also find small, round bare spots of dirt around while hiking. Deer also have scent glands just above their front feet so another way to mark their territories is by making *scrapes* with their front feet, leaving their scent as well as a visible mark to let others know they've been there—telling them to stay away!

Get out and follow a deer trail, especially in the fall. There are lots of fun things to discover.

Whitetail buck
(Photo taken at TNWR)

Chapter 43
"Oh, Deer—Again?"

(Winter)

As should be obvious with the last two chapters, our whitetail deer have a lot of incredible adaptations. One myth about deer needs to be straightened out, however. Most of us are going to look at the size of a deer's track and assume the bigger the track, the bigger the deer. This is not necessarily true, however. The track of a small deer in the mud or in melting snow is going to appear to be bigger than that of a large deer on hard ground or "cold" snow.

An adaptation that deer have while walking is to bring their back foot up to where their front foot had landed. This helps them walk through the woods more quietly as they can see where there front foot is landing, assuring a quieter spot, but not their back foot. Because of its length and stride, a large deer's back foot will often not quite hit the front foot's track exactly in the middle, but rather just a little short of center. A small deer's back foot is just the opposite, landing more toward the front of center. Look for the overlap of the track; if the top track is hitting the back, large deer, if it's hitting the front, small deer—if no noticeable difference, likely a medium-size deer.

The size of a deer does not necessarily determine age either. Size is much more determined by the general health and food sources of the deer. The corn-fed deer around here tend to be larger than deer in the north woods. Also, a deer will hit peak size and health between the ages of four and a half and six and a half, including antler growth. In its later years, the size, general health, and antler size tend to get smaller, as that is approaching old age for deer. If they are lucky enough not to die earlier, they rarely live beyond about twelve years. In fact, the average age of a buck in Wisconsin is only about one and a half due primarily to hunting.

The only way to get a fairly accurate age of a deer is to look at their teeth. They keep their baby or "milk" teeth until they're one and a half. At that age they get rid of these milk teeth and grow their permanent teeth. After that, if they are lucky enough to live that long, their teeth slowly wear away until by about age twelve, when they have worn down to their gums and will likely starve to death. During those years (one and a half to twelve), aging gets to be more of an estimate by looking to see how much the teeth have worn down.

The reason aging always uses halves is because deer are born in May and June, and most die during the deer season and winter at the age of one and a half, two and a half, three and a half, etc.

Chapter 44
"Giant Rabbits!"

(Spring)

While hiking at the refuge with my fifth graders one fall, I was pointing out all the various deer signs such as trails, buck rubs, scrapes, scat/deer droppings, and browsing. I mentioned that you could tell the difference between a deer's browsing and that of a rabbit's. As deer only have incisors with their bottom teeth, they can't "clip" off the twigs, but rather have to kind of tear it off. The twig is, therefore, very rough at the edge. Rabbits, on the other hand, have incisors both top and bottom so have a nice, clean cut of the twig, much like cutting it with scissors. We found examples of both so they could see the difference.

The following spring, we were hiking again at the refuge, and I had them watching for deer signs, including browse signs. They found deer browse and identified it correctly. They then found another browse with that nice, clean clip, so right away said it was a rabbit browse. The problem was that it was about three feet off the ground. One comment blurted out was, "Wow! That must have been a *huge* rabbit!" The arguments than began as to whether it was a deer or huge rabbit—or possibly that Mr. Lee didn't know what he was talking about, as there's no way a rabbit could be that big, yet it was clearly not browsed the way he said it should be.

After some discussion and reminding them of the very snowy winter we'd just had, they eventually deduced that this plant *had* been browsed by a normal-size rabbit, but it must have been during the winter while standing on top of all that deep snow, and hopefully, their most important deduction was that maybe Mr. Lee *does* know what he's talking about! ☺

Chapter 45
"Wow, Look at All Those Eagles!"

(Summer)

Quite often during the summer around here, I have people tell me about the big flock of eagles they saw, especially over the bluffs along the river. As nicely as I can, I inform them that, "You don't know what the heck you're talking about!" Well, I'm not really that blunt, but I do tell them that they won't see flocks of eagles around here during the summer. They certainly might during the spring and fall migrations, but not the summer. You can see flocks of turkey vultures, however. I then explain how to tell the difference.

While flying, bald eagles' wings are pretty straight out, while vultures' wings "V" up. They also fly as if they've had a little too much to drink, as they sort of rock back and forth in an unsteady kind of way. Also, the head of a bald eagle is much more prominent than a vulture's. It doesn't seem right, but the vulture's head is bald while the eagle's is covered with feathers. The bald in the name is from "piebald," a term used for an animal with white and another color in its markings, leading to their name. Their heads, therefore, look much bigger as it flies compared to the vulture.

The bald head of the vulture is an important adaptation. Their food of choice is carrion—dead animals. In fact, their idea of a good meal is by following the rule "the deader, the better," so their food is often already been discovered by other critters such as maggots. Imagine having a head full of maggots crawling under your hair. They likely wouldn't like that any better than us, so have adapted to having no feathers for those critters to infest.

Rotting animals, as you know, tend to get rather "ripe" smelling, so the best way to find that as a meal is to have a good sense of smell. The vultures nose is pretty hard to beat and can smell a good meal from far up in the sky. The thermals carry that smell into the air, and the vultures, often many of them in a flock, soar around above it until they can pinpoint exactly where it is. Those flocks of "eagles" being reported, therefore, are likely a flock of hungry turkey vultures. (The turkey part comes because of the red, bald head, which is similar to that of a turkey.) They dive into their food with relish, using their raptor (hooked) beak to tear it apart.

Their "neatest" adaptation was discovered the hard way by a friend of mine. He was exploring a little cave in a peak above Trempealeau one spring, a spot that I knew was a favorite nesting spot for vultures. When he crawled into the cave, there was an adult and baby vulture in there. The vulture's first choice of escape, of course, is to fly, but with John blocking the cave entrance, that was not an option. The vulture, therefore, did what vultures do when forced to defend themselves—it threw up/barfed/hurled/puked/regurgitated (I got lots of synonyms from my students) all over. Now you know how disgusting it is when you do that, so imagine what it would be like if you had been eating dead, rotten, decaying meat as your last meal. John told me he could not get out of that cave fast enough and nearly fell off the cliff in the process. He said it was the most disgusting smell he'd ever experienced. It's obviously a very effective defense mechanism for the vulture and was a valuable lesson on spelunking for John.

Turkey vulture
(Photo taken in Trempealeau)

Chapter 46
"What Big Teeth You Have, My Dear"

(Autumn)

As mentioned previously, the beaver has some pretty incredible adaptations besides dam and lodge construction. To cut down the wood needed for those lodges and dams, as well as for food to get through the winters, they have some amazing *teeth*. Imagine having to chew down a tree! It would certainly lead to a huge dental bill. They, however, do that with the greatest of ease. Like the squirrel, they are rodents, so have very strong teeth, which grow continually throughout their lives.

Beaver skull and jaw

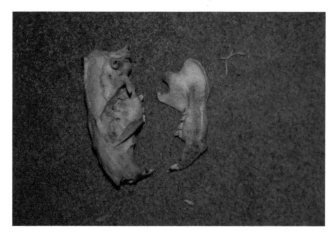

Their *feet* are also specially adapted to their lifestyle. The back feet are very large and webbed, enabling them to be very strong swimmers. The front feet are much smaller for use in hanging onto the tree while chewing on it. They also have an oil gland between two of their claws. While grooming themselves, they spread an oil into their fur, making it waterproof for warmth and protection.

Beaver front and back foot

Their *fur* is very thick and able to repel water—thanks to that oil. This is a great asset when you're going to be spending much of the winter swimming around in the cold water underneath the ice. Historically, that fur nearly led to their extinction, however, as it became very valuable to the early Europeans. They trapped them heavily and shipped them back to a beaver-free Europe where one of the primary uses was to make Lincoln-like top hats—a delicacy for the elite. Fortunately, some good conservation measures were put into place, saving them and helping them make a great comeback to where they are now.

Beaver pelt

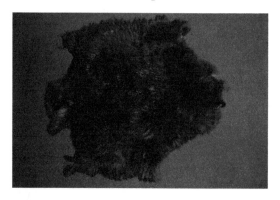

The *tail* is their greatest adaptation, however. It's a "rudder" for swimming, a "kickstand" to balance back on while chewing on trees, a "heater" with its dark color to absorb heat, an "air conditioner" to dip into the water to cool them off in the warm summer, and a "refrigerator" for storage of fat that it builds up through the fall and uses as a backup food supply to help them get through the long winters.

Beaver tail

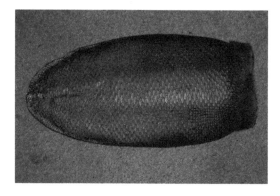

Epilogue
"Once a Teacher, Always a Teacher"

I retired from Trempealeau Elementary School in 2008 after thirty-three years. I still loved my job and knew I would miss it, but a change in my life factored greatly into that decision. My daughter had also become an elementary teacher, something she had wanted to do almost literally from the day she was born. She had taught a few years around here, but then had an opportunity to teach in Iowa City, Iowa, about four hours away. We hated to see her move so far away, but the worst thing was that she decided to take her four-year-old son with her—the nerve! He was our first and only grandchild at the time and, as she was a single mom, I had taken a pretty big part in raising him. He was my best buddy, and I couldn't get enough of him.

That year of having him so far away was really difficult, so I decided it was time to retire, giving me more time to make the drive down to see him (and also her, of course). I, therefore, turned in my papers and called it a career. Lo and behold, three weeks after I finished my final school year, my daughter applied for, and was given, a second grade teaching job right here at Trempealeau Elementary School. It was incredible! They not only moved back here, but even moved in with us for a while until they found a place of their own. I was better about letting her take Aiden with her on that move, as now it was only a few miles away, and I could be with him every day if I wanted (which I did).

I thoroughly enjoyed that first year of complete retirement but still felt I had some teaching left in me. An opportunity arose for a teaching job in the Environmental Studies Department at University of Wisconsin-La Crosse, only twenty miles from home, so I was back in the classroom the following year. I taught two, three-credit sections of the Introduction to Environmental Studies, with both meeting every Tuesday and Thursday. It was perfect—always a long weekend, lots of time for Aiden. I was teaching just what I loved teaching the most (nature and the environment), and a new challenge working with much older "kids." I spent the next eight years there and loved every minute of it.

I think I could have done that forever, but the time came where I had a "bucket list" to fill and needed even more time off to fill it. The year after retiring from there, I fulfilled number one—visited Hawaii, my fiftieth state. We're well on our way on number two— visit every national park in at least the Continental United States. I absolutely loved all of my teaching experiences, but retirement may be my best "job" yet. The pay isn't that great, but the benefits are magnificent. If only I didn't have to get old to do that!

I continue to "teach," just not in the classroom much anymore. I do programs whenever asked, which I love. I've created programs on unhuggable animals, animal adaptations, owls, snakes, and others, as well as lead numerous nature hikes, so have kept as busy as I want doing those around the area. I also now have five incredible grand-children and try to teach them about nature and our environment as much as I can. My kids do a great job of doing that themselves, but I have a lot more free time, so take it upon myself to keep on teaching, with the grandkids as my primary students.

I have always felt that teaching is one of, if not *the* most import-ant professions. All of us can and should be teachers in whatever capacity we can. Teach your children, teach other children, teach your friends and family, teach what you know best; and when you don't necessarily know the subject that well, learn it together. I personally feel that nothing can be more important than our environment. As without a healthy environment, what kind of future do our children, grandchildren, and future generations have? Go out and be teachers!

Special Thanks

There are so many people I should be thanking for what led to this book. I'll never get them all, but want to at least recognize some of them.

First of all, I must thank my parents, Arlan and Marjorie Lee. I think they would have been proud that I took this on, and certainly would have made me feel good about it, whether they enjoyed the book or not. Besides everything else, Dad is responsible for my love and respect of the outdoors, and Mom taught me the importance of teaching.

Cheri and Jane were my cohorts on my path of environmental education. Our time together at various workshops and conferences was not only educational, but a whole lot of fun. The three of us, with help from many others on the staff, led to a pretty incredible environmental education program at Trempealeau Elementary and even being named the top environmental school in the state by the Wisconsin Association for Environmental Education (WAEE).

Tom, the custodian at the elementary school, was invaluable in everything I did, in school and out, in nature education. He is the smartest person I know when it comes to nature, and our time together in the out-of-doors was always great fun and always a learning experience.

Ev, Marge, and Margaret, my three fifth-grade teaching partners over the years, made teaching not only fun, but also made it easy. They were all so good to work with, and I had very special relationships with all of them. They continue to be very special friends even though we don't get to see each other nearly as much as I'd like.

Wisconsin Association for Environmental Education (WAEE) was the most important organization I belonged to. I have a life membership, attended dozens and dozens of their workshops and conferences through the years, and always came back inspired to initiate valuable lessons and activities I picked up at them and from the many great friends I made through that organization.

The staff at Trempealeau Elementary School all played parts in making my career there fun and rewarding. I can't imagine teaching with a better group of individuals. Thanks to all of you!

I managed to take most of the photos, but if I needed a special one, I knew I could count on Allen Blake Sheldon, "photographer extraordinaire," to come through. He lives in Trempealeau, where most of his amazing nature photography is done.

Buzz, who was my mentor, friend, and office mate in my career at University of Wisconsin-La Crosse, assisted me with the knowledge and direction to take with college students. He always inspired me and helped me become a better college teacher. His students were so lucky to have had him.

The community of Trempealeau has to be the utopia of places to live and teach. Thank you for the support, patience, and providing such incredible children for me to work with.

Most instrumental in this undertaking has been my family. Judy, my first love and my wife since June 26, 1971, has always inspired, supported, and kept me humble (not an easy task). Other than not being real compatible while hiking, we have had a wonderful partnership (she's a retired physical education and health teacher, so she hikes for exercise, while I'm a slow hiker, checking out everything along the way—or at least what wasn't scared away by her faster pace).

My two children, Carne and Mark, were my constant companions on my hikes in the refuge, boat trips to explore the marsh, and wherever else my nature yearnings took me. Unfortunately, they grew up and headed in their own directions, but gave me five terrific grandchildren that have taken their place on those little trips. They continue to inspire me and give me reason (such as their children) to do what I can to make this planet of ours clean and healthy. Carne, who has a great gift for words, has also served as my proofreader in this endeavor.

About the Author

 Scott is a retired elementary teacher and environmental studies college educator. Growing up in western Wisconsin near the Mississippi River, he developed a love of nature early in his life. Having three older sisters, who led to eight nieces and nephews by the time he was through college, he also realized how much he enjoyed being around children. This, plus having an elementary school teacher as a mother, and a father who loved the out-of-doors, were all instrumental in the choosing of his career path.

Through his career, he has been honored with a number of teaching and personal awards. His first, and still the most cherished by him, was being named 1988 Citizen of the Year in Trempealeau, Wisconsin, the community he had loved his entire life and where he taught for thirty-three years. Through the years, he was also recognized with the following regional, state, national, and international awards and honors:

1988 *American Wilderness Leadership School* near Jackson, Wyoming
1989 Western Wisconsin *"Natural Resources Award"* (Wisconsin Department of Natural Resources)
1990 Wisconsin Association for Environmental Education State *"Environmental Educator of the Year"*
1991 Trempealeau County *"Conservation Teacher of the Year"*
1991 *Kohl Fellowship* recipient
1992 Cooperative Educational Service Agency *(CESA 4) "Educator of the Year"*
1992 Wisconsin *"Conservation Teacher of the Year"*
1993 Bridgestone/Firestone *National "Eco-Educator of the Year"*

1994 Roger Tory Peterson Institute *"National Nature Educator of the Year"*

1995 International Crane Foundation's Teacher Team Member for *Environmental Education Teaching Trip to Siberia*

He has felt so blessed to have the career he's had, having it in such a remarkable part of the world, and been able to work with such incredible staff and children throughout his career.

CPSIA information can be obtained
at www.ICGtesting.com
Printed in the USA
LVHW070506180621
690568LV00018B/1682